Principled Governance When Everything Matters

Principled Governance When Everything Matters

David S. Fushtey

edited by
Richard Littlemore and Moura Quayle

INFORMATION AGE PUBLISHING, INC.
Charlotte, NC • www.infoagepub.com

Library of Congress Cataloging-in-Publication Data

A CIP record for this book is available from the Library of Congress
http://www.loc.gov

ISBN: 978-1-64802-652-2 (Paperback)
       978-1-64802-653-9 (Hardcover)
       978-1-64802-654-6 (E-Book)

Copyright © 2021 Information Age Publishing Inc.

All rights reserved. No part of this publication may be reproduced, stored in a retrieval system, or transmitted, in any form or by any means, electronic, mechanical, photocopying, microfilming, recording or otherwise, without written permission from the publisher.

Printed in the United States of America

Contents

Acknowledgments vii
Foreword ix
The Reader's Guide xiii
Prologue: Since Machiavelli: Times Have Changed; People,
Not So Much xvii

1   Governance in the Digital Age 1
2   Governance Beyond Machiavelli 17
3   Risk, Diligence, and Best Interests 29
4   Consequences 45
5   Summary 63

    Biography of David S. Fushtey 77
    Notes 79

Acknowledgments

This book is a labor of love and respect from Dave's friends and colleagues. At Moura's request, the community of Dave's fans listed below offered up their time, expertise, and commitment to either (a) summarize one and sometimes two of the lengthy and complex chapters from the original book or (b) review this final short-form for content and style. In the era of COVID-19, several Zoom meetings ensued to debate, "What did Dave mean by that?" Each and every contributor put in an amazing level of detailed attention. The following people (in alphabetical order) deserve a huge applause of thanks:

> Karl Buhr, Gregg Birkenshaw, Elisabeth Cooke, Roger Courtenay, Colin Doylend, Cassie Doyle, Chenghau Du, Alan Duncan, Patricia Graham, Richard Hart, Paul Jorgensen, David Lemon, Norine MacDonald, Rajdeep Malhi, Paul Morford, Daniel Muzyka, Kirk LaPointe, Shirley Nakata, Marc LePage, John Nicholson, Michelle Osry, Shenaz Shahban, Marion Shaw, John Swift, Mary Lynn Young, Ruth Wittenberg, Anne Wittman, Tamara Vrooman.

Finally, a thank you to Richard Littlemore, without whose talents, patience, and sense of humor this book would not have happened. Thank you, Richard!

Foreword

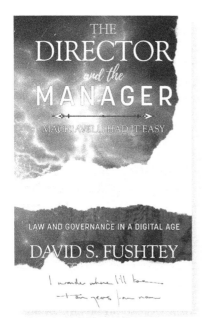

This book is a distillation of the wisdom and meaning to be found in David S. Fushtey's masterwork—*The Director and the Manager: Law and Governance in a Digital Era: Machiavelli Had It Easy* (Fushtey, 2019). While that 1,056-page text is already an invaluable guide for academics and governance theorists, it seemed clear that its insights and observations should also be accessible—in highly readable form—to all those who take seriously their responsibilities as governors, directors, or managers. Certainly, Fushtey believed that everyone deserves *principled governance.*

Throughout his life, David Stewart Fushtey played many roles. He was a big-firm and small-firm lawyer, a landscape architect, and an urban designer. He was a renaissance man who loved music, art, ideas, and argument and who found the time, and the need, to also build a business as a sculptor-in-stone. But for our purposes, Dave was a dedicated student and an expert practitioner in the field of governance. He spent decades conducting research and serving as governance counsel, during which time he developed a market-tested decision-making framework for the governance role, encompassing everything from comparative law and market practice to the vagaries, challenges, and limitations of human nature in the digital age. Dave spent much of his last 10 years thinking, researching, writing, editing, and compiling that framework into his magnum opus, published in May 2019 by InfoAge Press. *Machiavelli Had It Easy* is comprehensive and deeply researched, and it was a fitting finale in a life of reflection, innovation, and expression.

It was a *finale* because Dave, my beloved husband, died in October 2019 after an all-too-brief battle with brain cancer. Before he was able to distill his detailed text into a shorter, more accessible book, he was gone.

Dave had a "beautiful mind." He treated every situation as a learning opportunity and would focus attention on the person he was talking with. He studied Mandarin and Cantonese sporadically over the years and could surely be classified as an avid and tireless Sinophile. His favorite quote was the universal adage: "One is never too old to learn, and you can never know enough," which he always expressed in the Mandarin: *huó dào l☒o, xué dào l☒o*. He was a great mentor for students and young professionals and was always there for protégés, ready to share insight, work through dilemmas, and connect them to his network.

Dave had the imagination to come up with ideas and the humility and technique to test them against the data, gathering information and insights from a diversity of realms. In a complex world, in which so many of us have been forced to become *interdisciplinary*—sharing our skills outside our areas of expertise and connecting and working with experts in other disciplines—Dave embraced the greater challenge of being *transdisciplinary*, working at the edges, accessing and accommodating the knowledge and wisdom of many disciplines, and most certainly combining the critical and creative voices of law and design.

In his final days, I promised Dave that I would do my best to get his important messages out to the world, in a form that would be immediately useful to all managers and directors, new and old—to anyone who is on a board now or who wants to be, anyone who reports to a board as a manager or advises one as a consultant, anyone who wonders why the local elementary school, municipal park board, neighborhood business association, national government, multilateral organization, or Fortune 500 company doesn't function as well as it should.

With Dave gone, I sat down to reread his massive tome, which had permeated our lives for so many years. After skimming, scanning, laughing, and crying over the book (taking it just 20 pages at a time), I was more convinced than ever that its important ideas needed to be heard and reinterpreted by many more people, in a more accessible, shorter format.

I believed that an executive-length version of the book would be stronger if reviewed and condensed by a select group from Dave's incredible network of colleagues and friends, fittingly people with the diverse range of skills and expertise necessary to help make his ideas accessible to more than keen students of governance with strong academic bents. Before long, we had a team of some two dozen participants, many of whom are experts in their own rights, and all of whom brought deep and relevant experience to the task. I asked this team to write for a lay audience—not for academics, but for practitioners, directors, and managers who want to improve their performance and their understanding of governance. Accordingly, this book is written for people who might read 120 engaging pages—knowing there are 1,000 more pages on the shelf if they can't get enough. Lastly, I engaged Richard Littlemore, friend and trusted editor, to pull everything together. That was my smartest move!

Before I explain the structure of this book (slightly different than its parent), I'd like to include a few reflections on Dave's motivation for writing the original. Temperamentally an optimist, Dave would increasingly despair about the state of the world—a combination of profound moral outrage and a growing pessimism about governance, especially at the local level. His own wide-ranging experiences bore this out.

Dave observed that, often, the individuals who step into governance positions are not merely uninformed and uneducated about governance responsibilities, structures, systems, and practices, but willfully so. He recoiled at the notion of people who do not simply lack access to relevant information on effective governance, but who actually reject any opportunity to receive, reflect on, understand, and act on such foundational knowledge.

Machiavelli Had it Easy (Fushtey, 2019) was Dave's response to this willful ignorance. It lays out a clear and coherent approach that is not rooted in a specific time or organizational context. Richard Hart, a dear friend and one of the contributors to this new version, put it this way:

> Dave's original book is not a *what to do* in governance, but instead a *how to do it* and, especially, *how to think about it*. Dave believed that governance is an activity that one should approach in a principled way, guided by particular values. That principled approach must be undertaken consciously, intentionally, and deliberately, with a fulsome appreciation of the responsibilities one owes to serve the diverse interests of multiple stakeholders in the ways defined by a range of different (and constantly evolving) sources.

Perhaps most importantly, that principled approach must be made with both fierce determination and absolute humility. Fierce determination because, to be effective, one must exercise courage not just by assuming the mantle of governance authority, but by actually exercising that authority—making difficult decisions in a timely manner even in (especially in?) the midst of constant uncertainty... Absolute humility, because governance is an inherently relational activity: One's ability to effectively serve the diverse interests of multiple stakeholders over time is almost entirely dependent on the moment-to-moment quality of one's relationships and interactions with others, and on the quality of the information one has available at the point of decision.

In exercising principled governance authority effectively, every voice is relevant, but none is sufficient on its own. It takes a village, so to speak.

We are blessed, then, to have recruited so many villagers to this project, exploring, interpreting, and sharing the insights and encouragements of David S. Fushtey. We have also restructured the text to clearly set out Dave's 12 principals and to make the whole work easier to use as a reference and sampler. The result is a pleasure to read, a challenge to think about, and a handy guide that may grow dog-eared on the desks of a new generation of directors and managers dedicated to principled governance. Dave would be proud.

—**Moura Quayle**
Vice-Provost and Associate Vice-President, Academic Affairs
Professor, UBC School of Public Policy and Global Affairs
The University of British Columbia, Vancouver Campus,
Musqueam Traditional Territory

The Reader's Guide

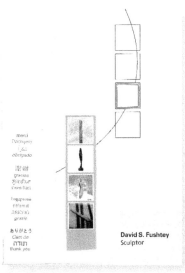

David S. Fushtey
Sculptor

Befitting the breadth of Dave Fushtey's vision, and honoring his inspiration, we begin with a prologue about Machiavelli. Dave was an eager student of the often-vilified political and governance strategist. He thought that Machiavelli set out some important principles that have often been misconstrued. So, while this section is not crucial to Dave's instrumental governance advice, we felt that exploring Dave's intellectual relationship with Machiavelli was a good way to set a context for Dave's governance principles in this complex digital age—a time when there is so much more oversight, responsibility, and accountability, so much data available, so many expectations. Indeed, it is a time, in Dave's neat summary, when *everything matters*.

Part 1 sets out the emerging discipline of governance in this age of complexity and makes the case for the importance of values and the influence of our digital world. Three principles underpin this chapter and begin to describe some fundamental elements of governance:

1. Know your role;
2. Choose authority over power; and
3. Respect complexity, embrace ambiguity.

Part 2 is about how people make decisions while "getting along." Three principles provide the context and practical ground rules for sound governance:

4. Act with integrity, welcome accountability;
5. Adopt respectful discourse and civility; and
6. Beware trust, common sense, and loyalty (the three horsemen of the governance apocalypse).

Part 3 makes the important point that good governance relies upon continuous learning, especially about essential topics such as the rule of law, risk assessment, due care and diligence, and civility. Four principles help set out key elements and approaches that must be weighed and applied in governance:

7. Nurture transdisciplinary thinking;
8. Take the time to acquire due skill, and to exercise due care and due diligence;
9. Reconcile best interests; and
10. Choose effectiveness over efficiency (get the right things done in the right way).

Part 4 warns that accountability attracts consequences, including blame and liability. It also raises the necessary place of apologies, and the constant risks of conflicts of interest and other challenges of trust and loyalty in the boardroom. Two principles are relevant here:

11. Recognize and manage conflicts of interest, and
12. Champion informed governance leadership for our digital age.

Part 5 summarizes governance competencies: "What makes us better directors and managers?" It is the practitioner's starting point, wrapping up the guiding principles in bringing intention to your role as a director or manager. These should be copied and posted inside your directors' notebook as a constant reminder of how to conduct yourself given the awesome responsibility and opportunity you carry as a director or manager of an organization.

Just head there if you want a Coles Notes of Dave's governance principles.

One other reading note: Dave used the terms *director* and *governor* frequently but not quite interchangeably, in part to embrace the full range of governance positions—including everything from corporate directors and academic governors to city councilors to higher level legislators. Here, as in Dave's larger text, the terms are intended to be inclusive: If in doubt, assume they apply to you!

Now, please enjoy Dave and his passion for governance.

Prologue

Since Machiavelli:
Times Have Changed; People, Not So Much

The great thinker, historian, philosopher, military strategist, courtier, political scientist, and, too often, cartoon villain Niccolò Machiavelli was an inspiration for this book. Indeed, *The Director and Manager* (Fushtey, 2019), the larger text from which this book is drawn, was subtitled *Machiavelli Had It Easy*, perhaps raising in some the hope that it would offer a broad critique, or maybe even a timely updating, of all Machiavellian theory. That was never the point. Machiavelli was very much a man of his time—and times have changed.

Yet, it is impossible to work in governance today without noticing how influential Machiavelli remains. In addition to being taught by philosophers, military strategists, and political theorists, Machiavelli's work is still cited as a guide for business—sometimes by those who appreciate the simplicity and clarity of his analysis and sometimes by those who embrace the relative amorality of his political and governance advice. The popular notion is that Machiavelli was more concerned with being effective than well-intentioned. But like other theorists whose work is often privately admired but publicly reviled, Machiavelli is probably more likely to be quoted than read—and, then or now, context is everything.

Niccolò Machiavelli was born in Florence in 1469, and he rose to prominence in the 1490s as a diplomat and military strategist in a republican government that reigned during a brief period when the powerful Medici family had fallen from grace. In 1512, when the Medici's military forces prevailed once more, Machiavelli wound up first in prison and then in political exile, where he began the writing career that has distinguished him ever since. His most famous work, *The Prince* (1532), is a slim volume of political advice that most scholars agree was intended to help him regain status in Florentine political affairs.

The characteristic that set Machiavelli apart, and that has attracted such controversy in the subsequent five centuries, was the independence and dispassionate nature of his analysis. In the early 1500s, most political writers were arguing that their patrons ruled by divine right, promoting the often dubious notion that nobility and "goodness" reinforced their claim to power. But Machiavelli stepped up as an historian or, as some have said, the first political scientist, applying empirical reason to politics. He pointed out that princes generally prevailed not by acts of God or grace, but by force, and that the precepts of nobility were often nowhere in play. Indeed, Machiavelli said, "My intention is to write something useful for anyone who understands it... to search after the [practical] truth of the matter, rather than its imagined one." And he warned, some say cynically, that

> a man who wishes to profess goodness at all times will come to ruin among so many who are not good. Therefore, it is necessary for a prince who wishes to maintain himself to learn how... to use this knowledge, or not to use it, according to necessity to secure his safety and well-being.[1]

Thus, Machiavelli counseled that the prince who hoped to maintain power should be willing and able to lie and cheat and to use violence, unpredictably, even to the point of aiming at his own subjects. Wherever possible, Machiavelli wrote, a prince should,

> proceed in a temperate mode with prudence and humanity so that too much confidence does not make him incautious and too much diffidence does not render him intolerable.[2]

But, the strategist added, ominously and famously,

> It is much safer to be feared than loved...for one can say this generally of men: they are ungrateful, fickle, pretenders and dissemblers, evaders of danger and eager for gain.... When times are good, when the need is far away, they offer their property, lives, and children, but when [need] is close to you, they revolt.[3]

The foregoing references begin to explain how *Machiavellian* became synonymous, not just with expediency, but with cunning, duplicity, or just bad faith. He certainly was not the first historian to document ruthlessness or to report on the brutal, mercurial and successful use of force and indirection. But by placing that analysis in a book of advice, it is as if Machiavelli invented the harsh notion of *realpolitik*.

This sense of Machiavelli as the standard setter for grasping power by whatever means necessary also sets some context for one of the references that specifically inspired this broader effort to describe good governance in a post-Machiavellian age. The story comes from Lord Conrad Black, himself a kind of 20th century prince. A Canadian financier and corporate strategist, Black rose to international fame—and *earned* his vaunted British title as Baron Black of Crossharbour—while building one of the world's most prominent newspaper groups. But he was brought down, prosecuted, and jailed in the United States for accusations of corporate fraud. (He was later partly exonerated on appeal and, more recently, pardoned, fully and personally, by U.S. President Donald Trump.) Recounting the details of this ordeal in a 2011 book, *A Matter of Principle*,[4] Black wrote about his dealings with the Italian business leader Gianni Agnelli, who had arranged for the Italian government to defray a large series of losses that Black's firm had sustained in a failed business deal. When asked how Agnelli had managed the financial manipulation, Black reported that Agnelli said only that he was from the country of Machiavelli, adding that, in relative terms and working in simpler times, "Machiavelli had it easy." Apparently subscribing to the dark view of Machiavelli as someone willing to take any measure necessary, and admiring Agnelli's updated skills, Black went on, "Not even Machiavelli would have had the imagination to devise some of Gianni's initiatives."[5]

Measured against the international forces arrayed against the beleaguered Lord Black, Machiavelli really *did* have it easy; in the 16th century, there were relatively few interests to consider and control from within fortress walls. There were no wikis to leak, no international digital databases, no informed activist stakeholders. In Machiavelli's world, so often defined by swords and shields raised in mortal conflict, there was no impartial rule of law, no recognized public interests, no laws of equity or negligence.

There were no public markets as we understand them today, no commercial rights, no codified human rights, and no international finance.

Yet, as the theorists and Machiavelli scholars have noted, while the world of governance has transformed many times in 500 years; human nature, not so much. So, there is, yet, insight to be gleaned from the classic texts. But governance—at least, what might be described as good governance—has moved well beyond the simplistic, self-interested decision-making that Machiavelli observed. Machiavelli's disjunctive approach of being feared or loved merely observed the value-proposition of the day: Conflicting interests were settled with a sword, long-term was relative, there was no objective body to scrutinize decisions and no rule of law to reconcile the better angels of our nature. In the time since, those tasked with settling matters of discord and dispute began developing ever-improving decision-making tools. Seeking consistency and reliability, judges refined the rule of law over 5 centuries of errors and trials. Regulators built systems to give order to communities and markets. Governors struggled to establish a baseline for integrity and values. And we now have access to an international digital architecture, giving us an unprecedented capacity to learn about our global village—and to be held to account on behalf of shareholders and civil society.

This modern, civil, and complicated governance infrastructure is, of course, a work in progress. But even while appreciating the clarity of Machiavelli's observations and the profundity of his insights, we would be missing a great opportunity—and running a great risk—to imagine that his advice about governance can serve unedited in this more complicated age.

Still, Machiavelli's time had parallels to ours in paradigm shifts of technology, a renaissance of beauty, and of hybrid governance as people of different languages from different principalities learned to get along. Although his practice points are dated, his approach prevails: He called upon princes—which we may interpret as directors, rulers, regulators, managers, or governors at every level—to clarify terms of reference, identify principles for application, and indicate standards from examples in practice.

In the first chapter of *The Prince*,[6] Machiavelli classified different kinds of organizations by three criteria of success: force, fortune, and *virtu*—although his *virtu* does not translate as modern aspirational virtue but as the skills to attain power. Really, none of these three can be casually interpreted or understood simply in the modern context.

Machiavelli would surely have considered force principally as the force of arms. But unless your day job is in the Pentagon, the modern manager or governor must be more attuned to force as the rule of law, for law is certainly the blunt force that governs our actions in the modern context.

Fortune, which too many market players might think of as wealth or, perhaps, good luck, was a more daunting notion for Machiavelli; it was chance or providence. It was uncertainty—that which could not be easily anticipated—and, in Machiavelli's view, if you were going to think about fortune as luck, you'd be wise to assume that it would be bad luck. Today, fortune might more helpfully be defined as complexity. Machiavelli counseled prudence and preparation, a bit of advice that Louis Pasteur later rendered as, "Fortune favors the prepared mind."[7] Today, the invocation of fortune is best understood as a warning against imagining that any problem has a single, simple solution. It's all about complexity and what we do to govern our affairs in the midst of myriad moving parts.

Virtu, however, remains the most challenging of these three concepts. In Machiavelli's view, it was not moral virtue, but something closer to prowess—the skills (positive and negative) that were necessary to attain and hold power. Some scholars have rendered *virtu* as courage and prudence, others as boldness—maybe, thoughtful opportunism. It might be stepping too far to assume how Machiavelli would redefine that notion in the modern context, but living today in a world with a nearly inexhaustible amount of information at his fingertips, he surely would have appreciated the virtue of learning—not just in preparation against bad fortune, but as the best opportunity to move confidently, even boldly, in whatever field of battle or endeavor you regularly must inhabit. Machiavelli wrote that, "above all, a prince should strive to give himself the fame of a great man of excellent intelligence," and, having lived five centuries before Twitter, he might have assumed that the best way to do so would have been to acquire "excellent intelligence" and act on it accordingly. But, per the note on fortune, it's complicated. Even today, with the machines and cellphone videos of accountability running 24/7, media and, especially, social media, seem awash in misdirection, if not outright deceit. There has never been a more critical time to constantly test the excellence of your intelligence.

There is no real chance, here, of understanding whether Machiavelli was a cynic and a villain, dedicated to seizing and holding power at any cost, or whether he was merely a cautious and alert writer of his time, noting well the dangers of always trying to play fair when others could be guaranteed not to do so. We cannot know, ultimately, whether Machiavelli was intending to write a handbook for being a tyrant or, as others have suggested, a guide to what nice people should learn from tyrants. But we can still find wisdom and guidance in his work.

Looking back on him as a progenitor of political science, we can credit his role in organizing the discipline of governance—of trying to understand and manage diverse self-interests, even in wartime conditions. And if we find that Machiavelli left aspirational conclusions for another day, the conscientious, law-abiding managers and governors among us can still take reassurance from his promotion of principled pragmatism, which would later emerge as the realm of the rule of law. Yes, he remains famous for his apparently low view of humanity. In his *Discourses on the Ten Books of Titus Livy*, he said, "This is to be asserted in general of men, that they are ungrateful, fickle, false, cowardly [and] covetous...and that prince who relying entirely on their promises and has neglected other precautions is ruined."[8] In *The Prince*, he wrote,

> One can say this in general of men: they are ungrateful, disloyal, insincere and deceitful, timid of danger and avid of profit.... Love is a bond of obligation which these miserable creatures break whenever it suits them to do so; but fear holds them fast by a dread of punishment that never passes.[9]

Even in these references, Machiavelli was a man of his time, relying on and, to some degree, parroting the great texts of the day. He was, for example, reliably well read in the works of the 1st century Roman emperor and Stoic philosopher, Marcus Aurelius, who observed that men were "jealous, arrogant, dishonest, surly, insolent, meddling, and ungrateful."[10] Even today, if any of us need reminding that humans are, well, human, we have a choice of 24-hour news channels to reinforce our understanding; but that lowest of lowbrow surveys needn't dominate our view or guide all of our actions.

Machiavelli wrote of ends and means in a time of battles, yet his conclusions indicated a strategic view in organizing governance decisions. He noted the importance of both audacity and learning to change. Machiavelli's statements were often simple and binary—black and white—but collectively his writing revealed an observer of more complex conditions. For example, he wrote,

> A prince ought to have no other aim nor thought, nor select anything else for his study than...organization and discipline; for this is the sole art that belongs to him who rules.[11]

Governance, in this characterization, is all about order and discipline—although, in the complicated present, it's never that simple—any more than it was in the sun-baked Tuscan capital of old. Indeed, Machiavelli sometimes referred to the regulatory organization of government as *ordini*, at other times, *arte*. In this, he seemed to anticipate the role of modern regulatory knowledge and skill, understanding that the need to organize and balance diverse interests would always demand a careful exercise of judgment. The challenge, now as then, is to learn the *arte* of good *ordini*.

Machiavelli also understood that even princes may be held to account, and he began (as an early booster of republican government) to ask how, why, and to what standards. Consequences, much later called liability, tended to be quick and final in the midst of a hundred-years' war. Machiavelli's times favored those binary and disjunctive descriptions: merciful or cruel, feared or loved, friend or enemy.

Perhaps anticipating the limited attention of his prince, Machiavelli didn't overplay his hand on this front, but he might reasonably be credited with introducing the concept of risk management by promoting two enduring practices: exercising prudence in the face of passion and learning from others' examples. He wrote, cautiously,

> Never let any government imagine that it can choose perfectly safe courses... because it is found in ordinary affairs that one never seeks to avoid one trouble without running into another; but prudence consists in knowing how to distinguish the character of troubles, and, for choice, to take the lesser evil.[12]

As we seek, now, to learn from the wisdom of others, we can also take note of Machiavelli's own notion on that count:

> For since men almost always walk on paths beaten by others and proceed in their actions by imitation, unable either to stay on the paths of others altogether...A prudent man ought always to follow the paths of great men...like the archers who...knowing how far the strength of their bow carries, they take aim much higher than the mark.[13]

This is not Machiavelli the dastardly courtier, crafting clever counsel on the basis of which he might reinsert himself into the halls of power. Rather, it sounds like Machiavelli the romantic, calling for prudence and urging the princes of his time—and perhaps the princesses of our time, as well—to aim high, figuratively as well as literally.

Finally, at least for this consideration, Machiavelli offers these points of superlative purpose:

> Nothing makes a prince so much esteemed as great enterprises and setting a fine example.[14]

> And nothing brings a man greater honor than the new laws and institutions he establishes, when they are soundly based and bear the mark of greatness.[15]

As we grapple with the challenges of governance and management, we should take heed of Machiavelli's cautions about human nature—about the efficacy of force, the fickleness of fortune, and the need for *virtu* in leadership. Equally, however, we may still accept Machiavelli's challenge to aim high, knowing that force is now moderated by the rule of law; that the winds of fortune can be understood and, sometimes, anticipated in the webs of complexity; and that the greatest *virtu* is knowledge and a commitment to keep learning, for the best interests of the organization and of the larger ecosphere in which we must all try to thrive.

PART 1

Governance in the Digital Age

Everything Matters: The Fushtey Framework for Principled Governance

It's like the setup for a bad joke: an economist, an MBA, a lawyer, a bureaucrat, an activist, a venture capitalist, and an engineer all walk into a room. But our experts aren't here for a punchline; they have come for a board meeting, and they could be forgiven for looking lost.

We live in a digitally amplified, digitally accelerated age of increasing complexity and unprecedented pressure—the pressure of time, responsibility, conflicting interests, and disparities in information. In this digital age, those disparities can make every other problem worse. We

Principled Governance When Everything Matters, pages 1–16
Copyright © 2021 by Information Age Publishing
All rights of reproduction in any form reserved.

all wake up every day with a cellphone by the bed, sometimes overconfident—sometimes overwhelmed—to think that we have every piece of information at our fingertips, even when we don't. We need a way to manage a breadth of issues that we can't possibly handle alone. If we hope to govern ourselves, we need a team of experts for support and a framework for how we can work effectively together.

We live in an age when everything matters, not just the obvious statements of profit and loss or of organizational purpose, targets, and goals. We also have a long list of other concerns, not limited to community and social responsibility, environmental sustainability, health and safety, public profile, and reputation. Modern managers and governors must worry about the crush of what they know and the potential impacts of all the things they don't know, yet—but should.

That said, *everything matters* is not an imperative to deal with everything immediately. Many of the weighty issues before us may not require innovative solutions. Many may be entirely outside of our control. But the phrase, everything matters, is a reminder that we need to pay broad attention. We need the skills, the patience, and the persistence to reconcile diverse interests and information streams. It's a variation on a theme of *assume nothing*.

> *Everything matters* is a reminder that we need to pay broad attention—with patience and persistence. It's a variation on *assume nothing*.

We live in an age when the calls for governance skills arise more often and in more places. Not long ago, if someone mentioned being on a board of directors, you might reasonably have assumed one of three things:

1. They had been hired to protect the corporate interests of a Fortune 500-style private business.
2. They were elected or appointed to participate in a governance function in the public sector.
3. They had volunteered to take responsibility for a board in the community sector.

In studying and developing the tools of governance, the academic and legal communities have tended to concentrate on the first example, the business company and its challenges in corporate governance.

Hybrid Boards

But things have begun to change. Responsibilities are expanding. In the way that people (and often problems) are the same everywhere, systemic governance solutions are both adaptable and transferrable. That's a good thing, because we also have seen an increasing number of hybrid boards that weave together business and community interests. Organizational methods and practices that began with commercial partnership models and trade cooperatives are now used and applied, for example, to strata corporations responsible for protecting private interests in a jointly owned residential property. These and other hybrid governance models, such as public-benefit corporations, are more easily adapted and adopted today, which means there is a larger community of people who need the skills and knowledge required to participate in effective and principled governance. There is, then, an increasing demand for people who

- understand governance as a separate discipline,
- define and clarify governance values for greater consistency and accountability, and
- understand and can design more detailed risk-management information flows.

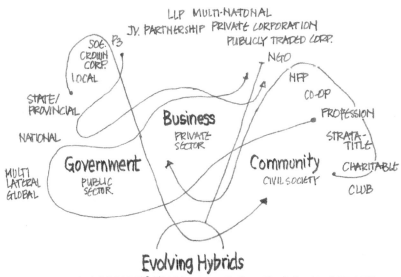

So, if you have come into the room feeling lost, or even if you have been a manager or a director for some time and still find yourself alarmed by the number of moving pieces and the breadth of responsibility, take heart. In the digital age—when everything matters—your concern and curiosity are your best defenses and may yet be the salvation of your board or organization.

What Is Governance?

Governance is a value-neutral word that can be defined simply as the exercise of authority. It is the process of reconciling complex interests through principles of law and risk management. But there is depth and complexity even within that definition and, accordingly, governance has emerged in the past three decades as a separate discipline, just as the formal discipline of *management* emerged in the last century and the law 300 years ago.

> Governance is the process of reconciling complex interests through the principles of law and risk management.

Academically, governance is now understood to require an interdisciplinary approach encompassing business management, cognitive and behavioral sciences, economics, engineering, law, and political science. Thus, it is increasingly important to involve a diverse selection of experts—and to embrace a definition of diversity that goes beyond job to include gender, culture, and race.

Effective governance provides direction on how to organize information—words, numbers, graphs, charts, and even audio data—and it does so in a way that, so far, cannot be replaced with artificial intelligence. The complexity and, again, the vagaries of human nature, are such that algorithmic solutions fail.

Governance literacy is also learned. The necessary skills of governance, and especially of strategic orientation and oversight, are learned, not intuitive. Directors and managers come from diverse backgrounds and disciplines, each with their own language and jargon. Lawyers, economists, accountants, and politicians view governance through their disciplinary lenses. But, again, governance is not only a concept of law or business or politics; it is a discipline unto itself, transcending fields. It is the specialized literacy, analytical skills and knowledge that enable diverse people to work together.

It's crucial to note, however, that while the word governance may be value neutral, the practice of governance should not be. The Bank of England and the London Stock Exchange spoke well to this point in 1992. Together, the institutions commissioned The Committee on the Financial Aspects of Corporate Governance to study the integration of business, public policy, and law—from which process Committee Chair Sir Adrian Cadbury concluded this:

> Corporate Governance is concerned with holding the balance between economic and social goals and between individual and communal goals. The corporate governance framework is there to encourage the efficient use of resources and equally to require accountability for the stewardship of those resources. The aim is to align as nearly as possible the interests of individuals, corporations and society.[1]

In 2014, the United Nations also weighed in, defining governance as "equity, participation, pluralism, transparency, accountability and the rule of law, in a manner that is effective, efficient and enduring."

Thus, we move from value-neutral governance to *principled* governance, which requires understanding and being accountable to the core values of an organization and a society. It is crucial, then, to begin with a systematic approach to identifying and defining the values against which assessments are made.

The Principled Governance Framework

The notion of a *principled* governance framework is not ideologically or morally based, but it is assuredly values-driven and has become increasingly so in the last century. In most cases, those values are also specific to the organization in question and must be identified as such by the directors and managers involved. Absent such a framework, any organization will wind up with governance gaps and hot spots—points of conflict or failure—that will undermine effectiveness, at the least, and expose the organization to extreme liability or crisis at the worst.

> Principled governance requires that directors and managers identify and apply the core values of their organization.

There also are principles and values that are broadly applicable and should be well-known to directors and clearly applied throughout the organization. The following are *12 governance principles* interlaced with key concepts such as *strategic oversight* that lay the foundation for principled governance. These are over and above the core values articulated by a particular company or organization and are important at a director/manager level.

Principle 1: Know Your Role

Every individual must begin here. Even aside from the diversity of skills, strengths, and experience that individual directors may bring, directors and managers face a huge amount of inconsistent information about their duties and responsibilities. Confusion reigns when roles are not clear. What am I supposed to be doing? What is my authority? Many risks and liabilities around the board room table originate in basic misunderstanding of "Who does what?"

Every organization should have a written description of roles and responsibilities for senior managers and for directors. Broadly, however, there are clear differentiators between the roles and expectations of managers and directors.

Managers or members of the executive must focus their attention on the details of daily operations and performance with a pragmatic priority on the short-term and on the well-being of the organization. Directors are responsible for strategic oversight—the longer term, strategic context—with periodic review and input on behalf of shareholders or key stakeholders (as in the case of not-for-profit organizations. Directors *must* recognize and respect short-term needs and reconcile them against longer-term, often-complex interests for the best interest of the organization and its ultimate owners.

> No matter how well-qualified you might feel—or be—in a particular situation, directors are never recruited to micro-manage.

To say again: the primary role for directors is always strategic oversight. Directors are never recruited to micromanage, even in management functions in which they feel somehow qualified. Management may benefit from their advice and insight, but directors must be careful to limit actual *direction* to matters of oversight and long-term strategy. Directors and managers need to respect and understand each other's roles and work collaboratively.

That said, even as the manager has a primary responsibility to the operations of the enterprise and the directors to strategic oversight, from time to time, they also must be able to collaborate across those roles. Mostly, that means that they have to communicate openly and listen to one another. The challenge is to respect the roles, duties, and boundaries of their own authority, such that everyone can do their part to deliver on the mandate of the organization.

Values in Law and Equity : Convergence

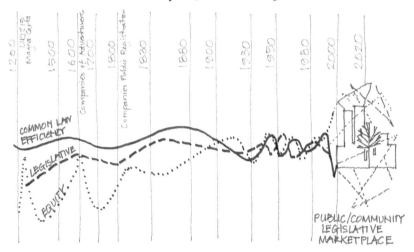

Values

With billions of people and hundreds of belief systems wired together in global marketplaces and communities of interest, speaking thousands of cultural and vocational languages with highly specialized words and different written and digital channels of communication, there will be much to learn and some to unlearn. Technology can sometimes provide the tools to do so; values provide the way to do so well.

Identifying and defining values is foundational to the governance platform of any organization. Values guide accountability and come in various shapes and sizes:

- *values of the quality of process:* deliberative, efficient, engaged, fair, strategic, supported and transparent;
- *values of the quality of individual conduct:* candid, honest, informed, learned, respectful, and unbiased; and
- *values of the quality of information:* accurate, balanced, current, credible, and organized.

Values should provide guidance and alignment at an operational and personal level. We have already spoken of the values in the United Nations definition of governance: "equity, participation, pluralism, transparency, accountability, and the rule of law, in a manner that is effective, efficient, and enduring." Businesses may be more inclined to focus on justice and fairness, even money and passion. The choice of values is important, consensus and transparency even more so. Everyone in management and on the board must know and understand which values drive your organization. In most cases, those values should also be known throughout the organization and should guide the actions of everyone from the CEO to the most-junior employee.

Again, over and above values unique to specific organizations, a principled governance framework should rest on a set of four core values and meta-values that should be kept in mind: four core values for a higher ordering purpose and two dozen meta-governance values. All need to be clarified by applied principles and standards and all will be discussed in greater detail later in these pages.

The four core values are

- accountability,
- effectiveness,
- integrity, and
- respect.

Meta values common to all principled governance include:

Accurate, Current, Candid, Collaborative, Honest, Committed, Consistent, Informed, Deliberative, Engaged, Diverse, Efficient, Enduring, Resilient, Fair, Flexible, Learned, Organized, Prepared, Profitable, Strategic, Transparent, Unbiased, and Useful.

People tend to prefer tangible problems, yet the words of accountability and evaluation in governance are all intangible. Each is a function of experience and learning. Thus, governance values are words of wisdom, literally.

Why Do We Need A Governance Framework?

A good governance framework is designed not just to oversee, but to solve problems that are multivarious and multifaceted. It includes the following challenges for directors and managers:

- *Lack of information and decision churn:* if information isn't flowing and decisions are around and around, like milk that will never be butter, it wastes everyone's time—and time is one of every board's most valuable commodities. Accordingly, manager- and-director orientation is essential, and this requires more than a skimpy board book with hard-to-read policies and procedures. Effective boards must devote time to rigorous board-member and management orientation to increase everyone's governance literacy. They also require "continuous learning" and an investment in board development.

> Good governance takes time, so directors have to invest time: Time demands on directors and managers, and related support, have more than doubled over the past 10 years. In the United States, corporate directors now face an estimated 250-hours average annual time-commitment—without chair, audit or crisis-management responsibilities.

- *Costs of noncompliance and disputes:* without a solid governance platform and high governance literacy, sloppy practice can exact real costs in any organization.
- *Lost opportunities and lost sleep:* when confusion reigns, miscommunication and lack of clarity abound, and we all lose—both opportunities and sleep.

These challenges demand a principled governance framework— improving our governance literacy in a very practical way.

Strategic Oversight

Strategic oversight defines the core functions for the role of a governor or director, clarified by applicable governance duties and values, for,

- setting values, principles and standards in strategic plans;
- ensuring that strategic plans have the necessary components to produce desired organizational results in a particular time; and
- periodically sampling and assessing operational and corporate performance for general compliance with such strategic plans.

Strategic oversight is more crucial than ever—and more difficult—in an increasingly complex digital age. Most directors serve only part time and may well struggle to stay informed, while executives and advisors, working full time, have deeper operational and specialized knowledge, and sometimes act as gatekeepers to that information. This puts additional onus on directors to ask questions of management. If directors focus on, learn, and understand the strategic-oversight role, they will be more effective in decisions on the values and information that matter, and, as a bonus, will help them to meet legal duties of governance.

> Strategic oversight should clearly set the direction, including by establishing and monitoring values and guidelines. Again, however, it is important to strike a balance, checking regularly on management, while still letting managers do their job.

It is particularly important that new board members understand and practice strategic oversight. This means that director education programs must focus on basics, including

- principles to guide decisions,
- guidelines for communication with stakeholders to avoid inadvertent non-compliance, and
- access to independent experts and opinions in dispute management.

Beyond the basics, the following are important tools for strategic oversight:

- performance-oversight panels, also known as accountability-oversight panels;
- anonymous and confidential reporting systems;
- compensation remedies such as assurance funds and agency-bonding; and
- alternative dispute management mechanisms, such as expert advisory panels (e.g., ethics or scientific panels), and ombudspersons in financial services and media.

Oversight needs to be consistent, not only for a sense of fairness but to avoid inappropriate risk-taking on the part of management.

Principle 2: Choose Authority Over Power

The purpose of legal authority in governance is essentially the identification, organization, and delegation of decision-making roles. Power arises from the people involved while authority is born of the rule of law. Power is taken or assumed; authority is granted by another. Generally, the exercise of power is unwelcomed at the board table in principled governance.

Power

Historically, governance relied on genetic predispositions of physical strength, cognitive biases, and instincts to seek or fear power. Before the rule of law, there was rule by force and many familiar mechanisms of power remain.

Today, power is often used synonymously in law and business, but there are clear differences. Power is not a legally defined concept but remains important in governance. Power can be considered a neutral concept—outcomes can be good or bad. But the source and use of power can be problematic. The exercise of power is essentially governance by personality or self-interest, and is limited by the influence and moral coil of the individual involved.

> The exercise of power at the boardroom table, by force or personality—or by shouting!—is never appropriate.

Shouting without legal authority, if it gets results, is governance by power; for that matter, shouting *with* legal authority is also likely governance by power. This is never necessary or appropriate in a boardroom.

Authority

To work more effectively with others, people learned to understand and respect authority, a process that largely evolved through developing a rule of law.

Legal authority is the starting point for how the law both helps and requires directors and managers to understand their roles in governance. This authority requires us to make decisions and, if we act in good faith, provides some degree of protection for us and for the decisions we make.

There is general authority—and there is legal authority. General authority is the right to make decisions and is usually granted by some other party, either by the state or by a private individual or group. Legal authority is the legal right to make decisions—most often, this is the type of authority that we talk about in governance. So:

> Legal authority, in all its variations and expression as rights and duties, is there to help people work together more effectively. Legal authority in governance is essentially the identification, organization and delegation of decision-making roles.

- Power arises from the people involved; authority is born of the rule of law.
- Power focuses on an individual and dies with the individual; authority focuses on context within a group and sustainable frameworks.
- Power is taken or assumed; authority is granted by another.

Authority also defines and bundles component duties for directors and managers which in turn include standards for governance conduct. That chain both triggers accountability and provides the conditions for evaluation. Authority is not intended as a limiting device, but as a way to help people work together, to define roles more precisely to avoid gaps, misunderstandings, and dropped balls.

> Principled governance requires a director to always keep these various forms of legal authority in mind to help stay within them and to know what is beyond one's scope. This knowledge will also help directors account for their own actions and better understand the standards against which their performance will be judged.

It is important to define authority and to clarify roles for greater efficiency and to avoid disputes among directors and managers and with third parties.

Also important is how legal authority is distributed to get the job done. In Western law, authority for decision-making is defined through what are called constating documents. These documents articulate a chain that is important for efficiency and effectiveness in both governance, operations, and risk management. There are three expressions of note:

- *Grants of authority*—an administrative certificate of registration that records the parties' agreement by legislation or regulations—grants are "steps in the chain."

- *Chain of authority*—each link of the chain represents a scope of authority and accountability. Under the rule of law, these chains connect governments to organizations and then to people, and back, from the people to organizations to governments.
- *Constating documents*—constating refers to constituting or establishing authority under the modern rule of law. Constating documents include the legislation, charters, and bylaws that provide the chain of authority and basic framework of principles and practices for such authority and to be accountable under the laws that provided the original grant.

Principle 3: Respect Complexity; Embrace Ambiguity

We live in an impossibly complex age. On any particular day, dealing with any particular issue, there may be too many moving parts, too many competing interests, and too much sometimes-contradictory information and *noise*. It is increasingly necessary, in exercising strategic leadership and oversight, to learn how to hold and be comfortable with ambiguity until due diligence or time constraints warrant otherwise.

Acknowledging complexity does not imply surrender or any abdication of the responsibility to understand and search for effective solutions. It's no excuse for untimely delay or dithering. Rather, it calls for prudence in understanding what is to be decided and in providing or moderating courage in action.

Increasingly in the last decade, complexity has been recognized as "situation normal," and more directors and managers are comfortable learning to move beyond the simplistic and easily known. Part of complexity is including multiple viewpoints and exchanges of negative and positive outcomes.

Although much has been made of adversarialism reflecting an instinctive survivalist *animus* in primitive societies, some element of the win–lose dynamic persists in modern society and in many boardrooms. Under the rule of law, however, the trend is that different interests can be respected even in a complex state of cognitive conflict. Indeed, other writers have described a "climate of optimal conflict" that can occur in healthy competition, in which you can avoid the extremes of complacency or rejection and loss of focus.

The ubiquity of complexity is apparent even in the careers of directors and managers themselves. Working lives may start in a company or not-for-profit organization, or in public service. Early experiences may be in a common-law jurisdiction, such as the United States, under civil law such as the EU or South America, or in emerging, hybrid-law economies such as China. Men and women may specialize in accounting, engineering, law, management, marketing, public policy, or any number of special interests, and they may speak one or more of several hundred cultural and vocational languages. As the Harvard Business School organizational theorist Jay Lorsch[2] has noted, businesses or organizations might also be collaborating or competing with multiple operations in several different jurisdictions, at the same time trying to manage the strategic and oversight decisions required for production, resource-allocation, and human resourcing.

In some regards, complexity has been embraced as a feature, perhaps even a benefit: progressive corporations have gone from reporting simple financial bottom lines, to triple and then quadruple bottom-lines. In some annual reports, you will find 7×7 matrices of interconnected risks and opportunities.

The rule of law has also evolved from a handful of principles to an ecological system of complex oversight. Leading international development organizations identify principles of governance that increase in detail with each updating (e.g., App. C18 re: OECD & IOSCO).[3] The problem is whether anyone understands what the words mean or, rather, whether everyone ascribes the same meaning.

Then there is the complexity of information itself. For example, in 2014, the member of a board that was contemplating a commercial telecom merger asked how many countries there are in the world and was told, in the lawyerly term, "It depends." Many sources say there are 193, which is the membership in the United Nations; but the CIA tracks up to 240 countries in different stages of self-actualization; and in 2014, the U.S. Department of State recognized 195. In the same year, the World Bank had 188 member states, and *The Economist's* Intelligence Unit tracked 169 countries.[4] No wonder, then, that complexity feeds skepticism of statistics in governance analysis.

Complex is also different from *complicated*. Complicated is something not likely to be understood though possibly respected as a knotted kludge of information. People can be complicated—unknowable personally even as we understand them as complex systems physiologically. *Complexity* can be explored and understood, inductively or deductively, and/or by organizing evidence. We are increasingly reminded of the fiendish complexity of systems and problems, yet have found that anyone can deal with governance complexity who has tried to explain good health, good golf, or financial derivatives.

Along with complexity, which can sometimes be conquered with more information, we also must deal with ambiguity, which sometimes reigns when adequate information is absent—or simply impossible to get.

Ambiguity is not wicked unless ignored. Ambiguity is not confusion. It is an interim state in a systematic approach to the quality of information. Accepting ambiguity in the context of larger information flow is another learned skill of informed inquiry: it is important not to hurry a conclusion but to identify the absence of persuasive evidence. Thus, moments of ambiguity are not so much to be feared as noted as occasions triggering further reflection on a board's responsibilities, authority, and duties.

> Ambiguity is not usually a threat, but it might always be noted as a warning—a prompt to try to do more research before taking action without enough information.

While the complex can sometimes be simplified, situations that appear clear in the outset can also give way to ambiguity over time. Consider, for example, Wikipedia's early ambition as a distributed, collective and open digital platform for shared information. It started with a highly aspirational regulatory governance framework, not unlike the informed and reasonable assumptions of the marketplace a generation earlier. Its approach was initially summarized and adapted in the tag, "Be Civil." This simple sentiment was intended to guide contributors, editors and readers around the world. Then tens of thousands of contributors started applying their own standards for what this meant. Wikipedia now provides several pages of detail to explain what being civil is intended to mean—in dozens of languages and hundreds of nations. Perhaps to clarify, Wikipedia now states, unambiguously, "We do not expect you to trust us."

As directors or managers, we cannot know everything—even when we know that everything matters. So, we must aspire to know our own role, to learn, share and be guided by the values of our organization, to understand and act upon the authority vested in us and, as directors, to exercise strategic oversight and restrain any tendency to try to do management's job. We must also guide our organizations to provide information that is as succinct and relevant as possible. If we can do those things, in a complex world, while embracing ambiguity and maintaining equanimity, we will have discovered the foundation of principled governance. It's a good start.

PART 2

Governance Beyond Machiavelli

Making Decisions While Getting Along

There is often a temptation, while running any kind of complex enterprise, to think that everything must have been easier before we had all these rules. Indeed, Conrad Black, a.k.a. Lord Black of Crossharbour—a corporate prince whose reputation and fortune are much diminished thanks to his own governance misadventures—once said wistfully that, "Machiavelli had it easy." The reference, of course, was to Niccolò Machiavelli, the sixteenth-century governance theorist who made himself famous by observing that governance success was dependent almost entirely on the capacity to wield power. An early advocate for the pragmatic ruthlessness we now think of as *realpolitik,* Machiavelli counseled that "a man who wishes to profess goodness at all times will come to ruin among so many who are not good."[1] So, he said, the prudent prince should conclude that it was better to be feared than loved—and act accordingly.

To Lord Black's point, the business of governing a sixteenth-century city-state sounds pretty simple: Impose your will on people whenever you can get away with it, and avoid stepping on the toes of people you fear. The problem for Machiavelli and for the princes he sought to advise, was that, under such a system, your ability to govern extended only as far as your capacity to enforce your will. Should, say, the Medici family show up with a bigger army, as they did, you could find yourself not in government but in prison, as Machiavelli did. It's true that he went on to write some very good books while in political exile, but he must have wished there was a better way.

The Rule of Law

In the centuries that have passed since Machiavelli's time, we have watched—and benefited from—the development and refinement of the rule of law, which the Oxford English Dictionary defines as:

> The authority and influence of law in society, especially when viewed as a constraint on individual and institutional behavior; (hence) the principle whereby all members of a society (including those in government) are considered equally subject to publicly disclosed legal codes and processes.[2]

The rule of law, properly constituted, provides a framework with three features:

- standards for compliance and enforcement,
- approaches to handling differing interests, and
- guidance for future conduct.

This is complicated for a prince—and sometimes for managers and directors. Thanks to the first feature, instead of doing what we want—exercising whatever power we have and taking advantage accordingly—we are now bound by rules with which we must comply, and we face agencies with the power to enforce and to extract a penalty in the breach. But the second feature offers avenues for dispute resolution that are less damaging than taking

> The rule of law serves us all because it binds us all.

to the physical or fiscal fields of war. And the third feature provides guardrails for consistency, reliability, and certainty, even in a complex and often-uncertain world. Together, this is where the arbitrary and often unfettered exertion of power gives way to the predictable application of authority and the rule of law.

Developed over centuries of trial and error, the rule of law progressed from developing a framework for legal institutions, to creating procedural systems, to aspiring to provide for substantive fairness. It was born of disputes, which over time provided patterns of conduct from which judges discerned common principles. In the commercial world, the courts were engaged to reconcile the drive for corporate and personal self-interest with the desire for efficient markets and effective communities. Specifically, this often meant trying to reconcile two core and often competing values: commercial opportunity and stakeholder fairness.

It oversimplifies to think of the rule of law only in the context of a judge and courtroom. The law also exists in ideas and systems: It is a framework to build ventures and markets, neighborhoods and nations. In the corporate world, there are now standards of conduct for individual directors and managers, for the board as a collective directing mind, for larger intra- and interorganizational relationships, and for stakeholders, like advisors, the public and the media. As always, the manager's priority is to keep his or her eyes on the road; the director's priority is to look to the horizon and the wider view for changes, risks, and opportunities. Both scales, however, operate within the rule of law.

Managers and directors should also be alert to the cultural components in the rule of law. Much civil law in the West is derived from the Corpus Juris Civilis of the Roman Emperor Justinian, c. 500 CE, which began to be adapted for local laws in Italian city-states by the 1100s, and later became part of codified systems such as those in France, Italy, Spain, and of their settlements from Quebec to Louisiana and Mexico to Brazil. The Napoleonic Code, introduced in France in 1804 and still in force, is an example of this. In Britain, a common law emerged, wherein respected judges made decisions that set precedents to be followed by all others. Even before Machiavelli's time—as early as the fourteenth century—the European, codified, civil-law began to influence the British, who started adding statutes and regulations. But you still have two fundamentally, or perhaps culturally, different systems. In common law, judges are bound by precedent and legislation, but have a relatively high degree of discretion. Civil law, on the other hand, tends to constrain judicial discretion through greater legislative codification. It's important, then, to anticipate that directors from different traditions might have different expectations and approaches to decision-making.

On one hand, then, Machiavelli *did* have it easy. The governance paradigm was less complex. That may help explain why, in the past century, prudent organizations have moved from selecting directors merely from within their social circles to seeking business experience, education, and diverse disciplinary skills.

But when it comes to managing internal controls in governance, directors and managers might still struggle. Judges and lawyers have the benefit of years of law school and professional practice to understand the rule of law and the administration of justice, to resolve disputes, administer records, assemble information, consider evidence and interests, and render decisions. Only in the past few decades have directors begun to have similar academic and disciplinary support, and the average new director would be well advised to turn to that assistance early and often when legal issues arise.

Finding the Principles in Principled Governance

So, now we have this higher factor—the rule of law—which is also a supportive framework, an independent control against wrongdoing, and a defense against the capricious use of power. There's every reason to hope that Machiavelli himself would have been less nihilistic—less *Machiavellian*—in his advice if he had lived within the protections of such a framework. But the rule of law alone is no guarantee of good governance or even good citizenship. In the governance context, it is not enough in planning strategy and weighing risk merely to obey the law. The intent of the rule law and of principled governance is to build great enterprises and set good examples, not just avoid risk.

The notion of *principled governance* also evokes more than a willingness to act on a set of principles—at least, if you define them narrowly as propositions that define a system of behavior or illuminate a chain of reasoning. Good governance also requires acting in a principled way, which the *Oxford English Dictionary* describes as "acting in accordance with morality and showing recognition of right and wrong."[3]

If you recoil at the word *morality*, be reassured. This is not an application of religious, ideological or even philosophical ambition. Objectively, managers and directors are subject to a whole set of legal and fiduciary duties, the purpose of which are to protect them and their organization's best interests, in the immediate and long term. That, for example, is why concepts such as good faith and candor now have legal meaning, even if the fine details can remain unclear. In practice, we may often find that it's easier to recognize good faith in the breach—as bad faith. There have been ample examples of corporate leaders who, by what they said or failed to say, proved less than candid, and wound up damaging the function and/or reputation of their organization and themselves. But good faith is not merely the absence of bad faith. It is the role of the board to establish the "tone at the top" by setting out and insisting on clear standards of conduct. It is in that context that the following two principles apply.

Principle 4: Act With Integrity; Welcome Accountability

Integrity

Integrity, while difficult to assess, is perhaps the most commonly cited morally desirable trait in business. Integrity is neither a classically defined moral virtue, nor is the concept systematically applied.[4] At the core of integrity is the idea of consistency—or constancy. This does not imply behavior that is static or inflexible: People with integrity may well be agile, respectful of diversity, and at ease with randomness and ambiguity. Rather, integrity promises predictable fealty to the fiduciary triad of best interests, good faith, and honesty. Within that triad, honesty is increasingly recognized as a personal value assessment with challenging cultural and vocational definitions; it lacks consistency. That leaves a fiduciary-like couplet of best interests and good faith.

Integrity applies equally to the individuals in an organization and to the organization itself, and it should be reinforced through formal and informal practice. Its value in governance is found in three quite different categories: personal values, governance processes, and performance outcomes.

Institutional integrity requires integrity infrastructure that identifies, organizes, and conveys information. It requires that your board endorses organizational values and codes of conduct, guiding and directing people and governance processes with oversight, compliance, and enforcement. Based on a system of values—normative definitions of positive interest and principles—its constitution and empowering legislation guide decisions on bylaws, statements of value and principle, governance roles, practices, and standards.

When governance issues arise, the public looks first to those accountable for whatever conduct and by whatever standards, and only afterward to values. Which is to say, the minute you step into a governance chair, you *are* accountable, which sometimes also means being legally liable. It's best to recognize and embrace that fact at the outset, tracking it in a way that means it will be an area of strength, not an avenue of risk.

Accountability

Accountability is defined as a process identifying responsibility, conditions, contingencies, and costs or benefits associated with an act, event, or omission. Properly managed, a system of accountability will identify costs or benefits and link them to the relevant causes or points of origin. A good accountability process should also identify or reveal potential negative consequences as liability, which is one of the great arguments for attending to accountability—anticipating the actions or inactions for which you or your organization may later be found liable.

The explosion of information and complexity make it more difficult daily to maintain clarity and efficiency, in operations and in the oversight separation between managers and directors. It's ever harder to assess risk and provide good feedback if you are awash in unsorted information—or are lacking critical data. A personal and organizational commitment to accountability strengthens integrity in principle and practice—contributing to fairness.

> Being accountable to others often means having to gather and attend to the kind of information that helps prevent troubles that might otherwise have been missed.

The effectiveness of an organization's accountability procedures may be undermined, or strengthened, by concurrent factors. On the risk side, hard-wired instincts, cultural biases, and vocational languages are inhibiting. Accountability's roots in numeric financial values and information can seed misconception, especially among those who are not confident in the language of accountancy (as opposed to accountability). This becomes another challenge for the well-oriented board, to bolster the collective knowledge of the mandate, mission, and operations of the organization that they are governing.

On the positive side, transparency enables access to information, supports informed decision-making and promotes stakeholder support. A board with timely access to well-organized information has a much better chance of conducting a fair assessment of governance decisions, more easily testing agreed standards of quality such as accuracy, bias elimination, completeness, comprehensiveness, and currency.

Wherever practical, it is also prudent—and can be helpful—to promote external transparency. It can reduce risk by inviting analysis and informed judgment by external experts and stakeholders, and it tends to limit overreaction if something goes amiss.

Governance represents the exercise of judicial skills, encompassing evidence-based contexts, values and principles, strategic risks and opportunities, and anticipation of future oversight. These skills bolster information assembly and assessment, decision-making, collaboration and cooperation, preemptive dispute avoidance, crisis and discord management, and long-term outcome effectiveness. They protect against the kind of information overload that can overwhelm a board's judgment capacity, lapses of which are often answered with counterproductive external oversight.

None of the foregoing is an argument to choose directors only from the legal profession, but all subject area experts should aspire to a judicious level of listening, questioning, and decision-making.

Accountability is fundamental to the art of modern governance. Its organizing systems, underpinned by technology, reconcile business priorities and risk. The aspirational side of accountability—improvement in both personal and governance performance—is of profound value to law and to good practice in management and on boards of all kinds.

Principle 5: Adopt Respectful Discourse and Civility

It is civility [that will] keep organized society from flying into pieces.
—Chief Justice W. Burger,
U.S. Supreme Court (1971)

Returning to the oft-maligned Machiavelli, one of the central criticisms of him and his writing is that he was somehow uncivil, and that he promoted or advised a kind of uncivil ruthlessness. Yet, the man himself might complain that the problem was not his lack of civility, but his critics' failure to grasp the complexity of his argument and his time. Indeed, Machiavelli was quick to warn of the risks of oversimplifying problems and solutions in the exercise of governance authority.

Surveying Florence in the sixteenth century, he warned of the difficulty of trying to govern a city-state of 50,000 people in the absence of common culture, beliefs, or language. In such a circumstance, he said, it was dangerous to focus exclusively on what he called one's "self-centricities." Assessing or trying to manage this diverse population on the basis of one's own perspectives, assumptions, beliefs, values, language, interests, concerns, and so on, was tantamount to governing with blinkers on. Such willful, even reckless, blindness to uncertainty and complexity creates yet more uncertainty and complexity. It becomes easy to miss important data points, to overlook problems or misunderstand them while trying to come up with solutions. And the tendency to oversimplify becomes both easier and more dangerous.

Thus, Machiavelli advised that the prudent governor should attend to other people, learning from them—contemplating different perspectives, understandings, and experiences. It's true that Machiavelli's motivations may have been tactical and utilitarian rather than compassionate and caring, but he still saw good reason to inquire into the lived experiences of others, to appreciate their "other-centricities."

If this was true and relevant for Machiavelli within the walls of his 16th century city-state, it cannot be less so for contemporary directors and managers, operating in the context of the global economy. Respectful discourse and civility are the bedrock of principled governance.

In his 2011 report, *The Charm Offensive: Cultivating Civility in 21st Century Britain,* Norman Griffith (et al.)[5] quoted a community leader who said: "We have to be polite because we are so different." Substitute "civil" for "polite" in this sentence and you have the perfect context for the need for civility in trying to execute effective governance. (Griffith and his colleagues also recorded the observation that the rudest people were generally men in suits, although other studies have noted that rudeness is gender neutral.)

Civility, with common roots like civil and civic, is all about people coming together for common interests. We think, today, of making contracts for trade, striking partnerships for commerce, or collaborating to build infrastructure or whole marketplaces. In antiquity, though, we might look back to one of the first public-purpose societies of common interest, the *societas publicani* of Rome.[6] Early in the 4th century BCE, that vulnerable city was saved from Celtic raiders by a gaggle of geese, which raised the alarm. Grateful Romans thereafter formed a *societas* to care for the flock, displaying a corporate foresight and betraying a degree of gratitude and compassion that might seem unlikely to anyone who has worked with geese. Still, as later *societa* were granted status to contract as independent bodies, the form would prove to be a consistent thread in civil society going forward. Who knew we would later raise a glass to the contrarian goose for its formative role in civil-society governance?

The call for civility—in governance if not in all of society—is tied to a core value of being respectful and observant of all governing protocols, laws, traditions, and practices. This imperative is all the greater in a global marketplace and in our own diverse society, in which dozens of languages may be spoken in a single elementary school. If boards are to benefit from the creative power of such diversity, we need to refine governance literacy for both vocational and cultural understanding. In this task, civil-society organizations ought to be the role models for reconciling diversity and complexity in governance, but corporate boards should also embrace the challenge. And in the governance context, civility must be both observed and enforced.

> A default to civil conduct is even more important in diverse social and cultural groups where misunderstandings might otherwise provoke conflict or dysfunction.

Of course, first it must be learned—and civility is assuredly learned, not inherited or inherent. One cannot assume that people will come to a board without inherent bias or places of intellectual comfort. Individuals may then default to their biases during times of stress or decision-making unless they have intellectual tools to do otherwise. Teaching civility means assessing risks of inherent bias/comfort, understanding empathy, and maintaining open-mindedness during times of crisis. It may also require reinforcement from a code of conduct.

When civility is left to informal learning or osmosis, the lowest common denominator generally dominates. Therefore, just as business standards and systems create a common understanding, so too should there be a way to teach principles of civility as an important foundation in good governance. The effort, however, can inspire arguments even in the orientation for a public company board. If a board tutor focuses on legal liability, then it's difficult to engender a conversation on the personal harm that might arise from uncivil conduct. But if the focus changes to the long-term effects of aggregated risk, operational effectiveness, or market reputation, then learning and relearning civility is fundamental.

Civility is the foundation for collaboration and deliberative dialogue to reconcile interests, and collaboration and deliberative dialogue lead to better board performance and outcomes. The willingness to learn can also overcome confusion that is buried in language or culture. And learning often means adapting when the commonly accepted truths of yesterday are upended by events. For example, the International Mercantile Marine Company share certificate once featured images of the Titanic—for a short time celebrating a culture of entrepreneurial spirit and courage, but soon becoming a synonym for misfortune and inattention to risk.

With globalization and digitization, the risk of non-civil behavior is exacerbated when definitions are not understood or widely shared, or cultural differences are not recognized or fully appreciated. In every context, we benefit by an ability to communicate and listen effectively, and in a socially and culturally diverse world, we can better achieve that advantage by learning and practicing a degree of civility.

On another note, Milton Friedman famously said that "the social responsibility of business is to increase profits,"[7] not denying the relevance of civility, but perhaps appearing to displace it as a prominent consideration. But Friedman would probably have agreed that corporate social responsibility must also admit of longer-term strategic interests such as reputation and social impact of decisions; these, too, have a capacity to influence profit—for good or ill—over time.

A lack of civility or pervasiveness of uncivil conduct is also more controllable in a boardroom than in the public domain. Modeling behaviors and being aware of others in small ways can be learned and practiced. This promotes cooperation and the prudent assessment of risk, resulting in better balanced performance of a board during a crisis, and providing better overall oversight. Civil conduct reconciles values, principles, standards, matters, issues, problems, and disputes. Intolerance increases risks.

Principle 6: Beware Trust, Common Sense, and Loyalty (The Three Horsemen of the Governance Apocalypse)

Among the values or constructs long revered in Western society, trust, common sense, and loyalty have been defining. But the real value in trust comes not from being trusting—which may be a synonym for naïve—but from being trustworthy. To be positive, trust must be earned, not given. Loyalty, as well. It might be appropriate that a leader, a manager, or a brand might command loyalty, but only after having won it through consistent strong performance. To *demand* loyalty is something different. People might reasonably question the basis for such an order. And what of common sense? On its face, it means assenting to what *I* assume to be true, righteous, moral, and sensible. But it triggers the question: "Common to whom?" In a world of diversity—and especially in a world that has often decided, for example, that Black lives *don't* matter or that women ought to stay out of the boardroom—a manager or director is best to avoid believing that their own assumptions and biases are commonly held. It's best to check.

> To earn trust, to inspire loyalty, it's best to test your own assumptions against the opinions of others in the room—and to ensure the room reflects reasonable diversity of people and views.

Yet the imperatives of trust, common sense, and loyalty have long been invoked to legitimize the ignoring, dismissing, minimizing, or denigrating of others and of their perceptions, experiences, values, interests, and concerns. They privilege the biases, prejudices, and internalized worldview of self over other. By extension, these same constructs implicitly perpetuate the maintenance of authority in the hands of the few and allow those few to continue in their privilege (typically framed as a right and entitlement) of prioritizing a narrow set of self-centricities.

History is replete with examples in which rulers have chosen to prioritize narrow self-interest instead of working to recognize, understand and reconcile the diverse interests of multiple stakeholders. There have been mega-projects in glorification of the sovereign at the expense of state economies, or wars waged to safeguard royal entitlements or avenge perceived slights to sovereign honor. There also have been rebellions in palace hallways and representative assemblies—and there will be more.

Whatever the sociopolitical antecedents of trust, common sense, and loyalty, these three horsemen of the governance apocalypse established firm roots in the governance cultures of Western corporate entities. Gradually weaving themselves into the fabric of decision-making conversations in the board rooms, offices, and production facilities of Western companies and public agencies, and of the various hybrid organizations that have sprung up in more recent periods, they have also been enmeshed in the language of court decisions, legislation, and the evolving "science" of business management.

But when trust, common sense, and loyalty foster in managers and directors' attitudes of dismissiveness, they simultaneously create and mask governance deficiencies and gaps. They impede access to reliable information and effective analysis. They block questions, requests, and demands for clarity, transparency, and accountability. They therefore increase the risk that managers and directors will oversimplify problems and solutions. The potential for associated negative outcomes is well exemplified by the major governance failures of the Dutch East India Company, Friedrich Krupp AG, Enron, Siemens, Bear Stearns, China Medical Technologies, and Volkswagen.

Managers and directors in the digital age have access to more information than at any other time in history. But so, too, do stakeholders, from employees, shareholders, customers, and competitors to regulators and courts. Acknowledging and tracking those stakeholder interests might create additional layers of uncertainty and complexity in terms of experiences, perspectives, concerns, priorities, and interests; uncertainty and complexity also arise in terms of cultures, beliefs, languages, traditions, and so on. But the uncertainty and complexity are there, whether you are paying attention to it or not. And traditions of trust, common sense, and loyalty are simply insufficient for and even harmful to the execution of effective governance authority by managers and directors.

By all means, aspire to be trustworthy. Do all you can to inspire loyalty. And do the research you must to understand as best you can the public consensus. Just don't assume that any of these comes to you by right, or that trust and loyalty should ever displace objective due diligence.

PART 3

Risk, Diligence, and Best Interests

Good Governance Is a Product of Continuous Learning

There is a world of difference between common sense and common knowledge. The first is an invitation to leap to a self-satisfying conclusion. The second is a reminder to do your research—to satisfy yourself that your assumptions are adequately supported by the evidence. In your personal life, the latter reminder might seem so obvious as to be banal: it is only prudent to direct and manage your affairs based on the best information available. As Machiavelli might note, just because you don't go looking for trouble doesn't mean that trouble isn't lying in wait. If, however, you have been promoted to management or recruited as a director, the common onus of prudence quickly turns into a legal duty of care. Over the centuries, courts and regulators have recognized the responsibilities of those in governance authority and, on an increasing number of occasions, have held managers and directors liable for errors, omissions, accidents, or disasters that might have been avoided with the exercise of an appropriate amount of attention: due care. Of particular importance is the underlying obligation of due diligence: the duty to inquire, to question, to interrogate—diligently until satisfied. The duty is also said to reawaken as new information becomes available. Due diligence needs to be deliberative and evergreen.

The good news for the diligent director or manager is that exercising the duty of care offers a double benefit: practically, it bolsters confidence in decision-making, and legally, it provides a protective shield against liability. Directors are expected to pay attention, but they are not expected to know it all.

This, then, invokes the related category of due skills. The successful—and legally defensible—governor requires the cognitive capacity and skills to observe and scan information for gaps, to take the time to exercise the care of a disciplined mind, and then to have the courage to either ask more questions or move to the decision stage. This last point, knowing when to ask questions diligently, and when to stop questioning and make a decision, is central to the realm of business judgment and to appropriate oversight.

Principle 7: Nurture Transdisciplinary Thinking

The foundation, in this discussion and in governance writ large, is the responsibility, the opportunity—the imperative—of continuous learning. The Mandarin proverb, *Huó dào lăo, xué dào lăo,* tells us, "You are never too old to learn, and you can never know enough." And if the latter half of the sentence makes you nervous, then you have understood the proverb correctly. It is impossible in the digital age, when we have access to more information than we can reasonably digest or understand, to fully inform ourselves. In the context of a modern board, where directors are called upon to sort out the complexities of finances, law, operations, risks, and opportunities, we can never know enough—so we need to know who does. That's why a well-balanced board will have a diversity of subject area experts among its directors. It's also why we all need to nurture the skills of transdisciplinary thinking.

There is a fine and necessary balance to be struck here. Consider, first, the definition of "interdisciplinary," which requires that we can work with other disciplinary experts on complex projects. This means recognizing expertise and trusting the skills, knowledge and, sometimes, wisdom of experts outside our own fields. It also means working with them in good faith, such that they can trust and rely upon our input. But it's not enough, in principled governance, to accept the advice of others as if it were delivered from some impenetrable black box. We all have a responsibility to meet at the edges, to do all that we can to bridge the gaps between our disciplines. In science and research, some of the best discoveries and innovations currently come in these liminal spaces. In governance, some of the most potent risks arise when the advice from one expert is misunderstood as it is applied—even in intended good faith—by others. Transdisciplinary thinking does not require that you become an expert in everything. But it implies a heightened degree of attention when you are working outside, or at the edge of, your own area. It means that instead of tuning out during the report from a special committee outside your field, that you should be listening harder. You need to learn enough to understand what you don't know; that's where you'll find all the good questions.

> Interdisciplinary is the ability to work with others often on complex projects; transdisciplinary engages a set of specialized systems and skills to work with diverse disciplines, in the best interests of something unique.

Principle 8: Take Time to Acquire Due Skill, and to Exercise Due Care and Due Diligence

For more than half a century—since Watergate investigator Senator Howard Baker, Jr. asked the question, "What did the President (Nixon) know and when did he know it?"—there has been a mistaken impression that ignorance, if not bliss, was at the very least exculpatory. If you could argue that you weren't in the loop, you might also make the case that you weren't responsible; you certainly couldn't be blamed in the cover-up. This kind of flawed thinking can create all manner of problems for directors and managers who misunderstand their legal duties. If the duties—and the details—seem to be complex or constraining, some directors and managers may seek to wrap themselves in a cocoon of time constraints and hide behind a curtain of complexity. As a risk-management strategy, this is analogous to walking through bear country wearing a bee-keeper's veil, lightly soaked in honey; it's a defensive strategy almost perfectly designed to get you into more trouble. Ignorance is *not* bliss. You can't protect yourself against risks you can't see. But, as the dutiful director soon learns, if you carry those little bells—which is to say, if you exercise even the base level of precautionary planning—most bears will leave you alone.

Governance duties have traditionally been described as fiduciary duties and duties of care.

- Fiduciary duties arise from a fiduciary relationship, commonly, between a trustee and beneficiary, guardians and wards, lawyers and clients, investment corporations and investors, and corporate board members and shareholders. The actual duties, if legally enforceable, still tend to be intangible: to act honestly, in good faith and in or with a view to the best interests of the beneficiaries, measured by the discretionary standard of the court of the day.
- Duties of care, on the other hand, can be visualized as actions, assets, or information: they are to use due skill, and to act with due care and due diligence.

This history of an assumed burden of care traces back to the time of Aristotle, who noted that ignorance through carelessness should not be excused when it is within one's power not to be ignorant "since they have the power of taking care" by being duly informed.[1] The Romans took a step further to suggest that a higher standard of more exacting care was needed in managing the lives or assets of others.[2]

The modern duty of care is a relatively recent development. An earlier tradition linking damages with consequences was developed into a duty of care in the nineteenth century after a critical mass of disputes and cases built up. The common remedies in these cases were then recognized and augmented with guidelines, which became defined as a duty to prevent harm.[3] Two landmark cases are credited with beginning the modern age in the law of negligence. In a U.S. case, McPherson vs. Buick Motors (1916), the plaintiff was injured when a defective wheel broke off his new car. The retailer blamed the defect on another manufacturer, but the court said that if a product could reasonably be expected to be dangerous if negligently made, then a re-seller had a duty of care. A second case, in the U.K. in 1932, involved the "Paisley snail." A Mrs. Donohue, from Paisley, Renfrewshire, fell ill after drinking ginger beer from a bottle that was later found to contain a dead snail. When she sued, the House of Lords held that the manufacturer owed a duty of care to her, which was breached, because it was reasonably foreseeable that failure to ensure the product's safety would lead to harm to consumers. This is defined in law as a breach of a legal duty of care. From food to pharmaceuticals, from engineering to the environment, the global village would never be the same as this updated doctrine of a duty of care was tested and accepted in principle and continually refined in practice around the world. Again, the caution is that the legal principles frame the idea, but details and standards vary by time and place.

The duty of care is a label used to bundle several component duties, which are generally accepted as the legally enforceable obligations to use due skill, care, and diligence measured by the standards of the day:

- *due skill* is learned knowledge and technique, currently including the obligations for continual updating of strategic oversight and judgment skills;
- *due care* is taking the time to be informed, reflect, and consider, including the obligation to establish internal controls, and;
- *due diligence* is persistence in inquiry, knowing the importance of being informed, and using internal controls to do so.

There are some clarifications and protections inherent in this list. First, "due" means the standards are relative, but even those educated in the skills of making judgments need more to go on. Legally, then, a standard developed in which performance would be measured against the actions of a reasonable person of similar position, in similar circumstances. This became known as the objective standard, inspired by judges looking at how highly subjective, personal views of blame were not working. The language of "reasonable" is yet imperfect, but still helps people make more informed decisions in their roles of director, risk-manager, regulator, or journalist.

Further qualifying reasonableness, the courts looked to the context of time, place, and people. This is vital in a global marketplace in a digital age when the relevant information changes daily. It also suggests another distinction between the roles of managers and directors. A manager needs to be compliance focused, not short-sighted, but necessarily attentive to what is reasonable and permissible today. A director needs to look at what will be reasonable, likely, and risk-conscious tomorrow.

The duty of care also is part of a web of accountability, which now includes trial-by-press and international reciprocity or enforcement conventions. These developments will then inform future judges' assessments of the relative standards of care that should be reasonably expected. An example is when directors and managers at Union Carbide in Midland, Michigan were held to scrutiny by arguments in the press for the health and safety of 1984 chemical spill in Bhopal, India (Union Carbide, 1984/2014). The case illustrated the expansion of accountability beyond borders and beyond financial liability to reputational damage, showing how much the global village is shrinking when it comes to duties of care in governance and compliance matters.

The scope of people involved is also widening. Directors and officers are increasingly being found to owe a duty not just to shareholders, but also to fellow directors, multiple shareholder classes, secured creditors, employees, the environment, and public markets. Increasingly, the only way to survive is to understand the complexity, and get out in front to avoid or mitigate surprises.

The duty of care applies both outward and inward, carrying both responsibility and liability. In another distinction between the management and governance levels, managers are more likely to enjoy protection from corporate veils of limited liability and business judgment, while directors or executives in a fiduciary capacity are more likely to be at risk, especially as regulators and legislators rise more aggressively in defence of the public interest.

Due Skill

Due skill, as the first of three components, is relative to the context and conduct expected. For example, in the professions, evidence of due skill moved from skills acquired by practical apprenticeship or mentorship and experience, to skills acquired through theoretical and applied knowledge requiring a university degree in a subject area as the sheer volume of information and standards rose.

In this context, "due" is defined to mean that the person's skill level meets the standards expected in law. In governance this could be technical, clerical or professional. For professionals in the twentieth century, this initially meant earning the degree, passing the entry exams, and then exercising common sense. Now, professional associations and courts have revised the standard to one of "over-the-bar-with-continual-improvement." When the public interest, health, and welfare rely upon certain standards of conduct or production, common sense is not sufficient. If you have been recruited to a board because of your credentials, say, in law or accounting, the stakeholders—and the law—expect that you will bring and will apply a degree of skill that is uncommon. Indeed, you have a duty to do so.

An example of due skill in governance can be found in the modern expectations of financial literacy and expertise for directors and officers. Once informally assumed, such skill was found lacking in patterns of mistakes and failures. It took the markets two-hundred years to define financial literacy in corporate governance; legislation such as *Sarbanes-Oxley* (2002), and the *Dodd-Frank Wall Street Reform and Consumer Protection Act* (2010) created obligations for governors to be financially literate, and defined *financial literacy* for U.S. and related markets as being able to read and understand financial statements appropriate for the type of organization governed. The new laws and resulting regulation ultimately required that boards or their management also exercise adequate skills of communication. They upgraded disclosure regulations not just for financial particulars, but for general accessibility of information and other issues of importance, such as conflicts of interests.

Due Diligence: Asking Questions

Most governance gaffes and crises are avoidable. Indeed, ninety-nine percent of legal disputes seem to arise from a lack of information by one or more parties, or a lack of consensus on the relative importance of outstanding issues. Judges have noted that skills of inquiry would go a long way to correcting such information deficits and have proposed the duty of care as a principle to help. From that flows the legal doctrine of due diligence.

The problem, at the average board table, is in overcoming the sense that asking questions is boring, expensive, and time-consuming. Another problem is that due-diligence practice guides and checklists abound, but due diligence remains an expression often used and rarely defined. The result is that different people will hear different things:

- Professional conduct experts should understand due diligence as part of the high standards of a legal duty of care for professionals.
- Corporate or commercial lawyers should understand due diligence as part of the governance duties of care on directors' decision-making.
- Business executives or managers in deal-making may understand due diligence as an expected box to tick in getting a deal done.
- Risk managers should understand due diligence as fundamental both for information assembly but also for the duty of good-faith and disclosure.

- Individuals responsible for future performance, whether regulators, directors of acquired or merged enterprises, or compliance officers, understand that due diligence is critical to support regulatory and legal standards and strategic planning.
- Fellow directors and managers should understand due diligence to be all of the above and also an essential practice for internal board effectiveness.

In exercising due diligence in governance, there is no common sense and there are no stupid questions, but there are respectful ways of proceeding. Due diligence requires being persistent, but respecting others by learning to ask questions first to identify personal gaps and to seek personal upgrading. That means preparing well, listening to others, and learning where to find or gain access to information. It requires learning and practicing respectful ways to ask questions in and out of meetings. It also requires the skill and determination to escalate questioning when urgent, or to table issues for further review when the answers do not satisfy.

It's important to remember that these legal duties did not evolve and survive merely for judges to analyze disputes and crises; they are aspirational guidelines for governance conduct in the marketplace. This cornerstone function is consistent with the transdisciplinary nature of governance, consistent with studies in psychology which have noted that wisdom is being able to ask questions, then,

- to act on that information, even while understanding that it may still be incomplete or incorrect; and
- to listen, consider the advice of, and learn from others, admit mistakes, and acknowledge complexity.

The professions learned early that skills of due diligence are not intuitive, but learned. *Diligence* is commonly defined as a persistent effort; in governance it means persistent effort to be informed. To do so well requires focus and time to learn and practice.

Due diligence is now a basic safety net in risk analysis and liability. Great lists are used to inform and confirm strategic plans, operations, and assets and liabilities; secure digital information systems are engaged to make it happen. Due diligence starts by taking an information inventory prior to decisions, including the diverse interests possibly involved. This becomes a strategic frame for operational decision-making, to get things done right the first time, consistent with desired long-term values.

Due diligence should not be confused by those who advocate curiosity as a governance duty nor passive monitoring as a governance role. The principle should not be abused to grind decision-making to a halt by seeking perfect information. The applied principle requires learning disciplined skills to assemble and assess information, leverage the technology of the day for informed decision-making, and avoid death by a thousand cuts afterwards or in the extreme, catastrophic loss.

The alternative is to risk passive redundancy, as when directors were perceived as and relegated to being passive figureheads as "ornaments on the company Christmas tree," or, in the U.S. vernacular of the 1980s, "pet rocks."[4] Board directors for much of the past hundred years were expected by managers, and some judges, to be pleasant if incompetent amateurs for whom onerous standards would be unreasonable and would deter others from agreeing to serve.[5] At one time, directors were respected for coming from diverse backgrounds but not required to bring any special qualifications to the table, and traditions of common sense and trust were expected. Now governance education or experience is largely mandatory, often a matter of compliance, and even higher standards of director professionalism have been raised.

Today, regularly scheduled programs of inquiry should include annual reviews, and a watch-list updated annually or as required in response to new information, problems, or crises. Information must be both current and credible, which requires asking:

1. "What is the source and basis of the information and analysis?"
2. "What are the reasons to doubt the honesty or integrity of the source, including bias and risks of conflicting interests or bad faith?"
3. "Was the information comprehensive, accurate and complete and if not, did the source identify gaps?"[6]

In governance, the systems required to answer these questions are often referred to as *internal controls*. The classic judicial statement of the modern era on this point does not focus on simplistic control but on effectiveness:

> Assure that information and reporting systems exist in the organization that are reasonably designed to provide to senior management and to the board itself timely, accurate information sufficient to allow management and the board, each within its scope, to reach informed judgments concerning both the corporation's compliance with law and its business performance.... [I]t is important that the board exercise a

good faith judgment that the corporation's information and reporting system is in concept and design adequate to assure the board that appropriate information will come to its attention in a timely manner as a matter of ordinary operations.[7]

Due-diligence systems are the core and future of quality management, risk management, internal controls, and integrated governance systems. Operating in a global village in a digital era, directors and managers need to get up to speed, together, quickly. The more complex the context, the more critical are good frameworks and information supply chains. Perhaps the greatest recent contribution to good governance has been to support governors around the board table through the technology and a culture of learning. Due skill, care, and diligence is increasingly embedded in continuing education and development practices, and it is expected of directors of publicly traded companies and hybrid boards and becoming more common for all directors and managers.

Principle 9: Reconcile Best Interests

If a duty of care compels governors to gather and analyze information, the next challenge is finding an effective screen or filter through which to make sense of that intelligence. Arguably, the best of those screens is the best-interest doctrine, an increasingly refined process perfectly suited to the age of complex, hybrid organizations of public, private, and/or special interests.

Modern managers and directors operate in a blizzard of self-interest, special interests, public interests, and private interests. The best-interests doctrine emerged in equity, a branch of law that was conceived hundreds of years ago by judges who were considering the diverse and increasingly complex interests of organizations. At the root of equity is the concept of fairness. As the modern study of governance emerged, hybrid organizations were few. Now every organization is a hybrid, reconciling complex interests. Profit-interested businesses are held to increasing social and environmental long-term obligations, while traditional

> The best-interests doctrine captures the need to identify relevant interests, identify organizational priorities and contexts, and reconcile the different interests involved.

nonprofits are now not-for-profit enterprises held to high standards of fiscal responsibility.

The best-interests doctrine anticipates identifying a broad set of relevant organizational interests which today include the interests of shareholders or members, management, and employees, as well as commercial, special, and public interests. Best interest also provides an analytical frame for concepts of fairness, fiduciary duty, and integrity.

When directors come from diverse backgrounds, education, experience, and expectations, they may lack a clear understanding of their new role or governance duties in law, and they may not yet have the skillset for strategic oversight.

The best-interest approach started with an innovative, intangible tool: the legal interest, a concept born in the old courts of equity to create an enforceable legal right. The interest is a basic metric of measurement and a fundamental tool for building and maintaining principled decision-making structures. It is an analytical unit that, while intangible, has proved to be flexible and scalable from self-interest to special interests to public interests. In governance, interest is a word that spans extremes in meaning from merely personal desires to something enforceable in law. A passing interest can mature into a legal interest and a legal interest into a legal right. The start in any best-interest analysis is therefore to cast the net widely to identify and organize a baseline inventory of interests. To begin, an interest is an indicator of a relationship of someone to something, or to some other person(s).

The skills and knowledge required to analyze best interests are fundamental for good governance yet need to be learned. It is not easy to set aside self-interest and special interests. Exercising good judgment reconciles complex interests for the long term, but this is not something most people do often. In governance, it is expected—and required.

Reconciling Interests

Best interests describes a process of reconciling myriad interests—and, to be clear, *reconciling* differs from *balancing* interests. The latter may imply that all interests must be included in each solution, whereas reconciling allows for situations when one or another interest

> Best interests in law and equity refers to the process, not the outcome.

may justifiably prevail. Still, a best-interest analysis—anticipating short-, mid-, and long-term scenarios—will consider and respect all interests, leading to an informed judgment on which interests get priority.

Best-interest analysis sets a proper tone—for strategic planning and oversight—by providing an organizing frame to

- avoid conflicting or confusing language of public, private, special, or civil society groups;
- identify stakeholder classes and their interests; and
- prime further inquiry for interests unique to the organization or context.

Shareholder interests will always be significant in an assessment of best interests. The challenge is to better reconcile other interests recognized in equity and law. By legislation, these may extend beyond shareholders to the interests of employees, retirees and pensioners, creditors, consumers, and governments, as well as of the environment—and the long-term interests of the corporation itself. The Treadway Commission (1987) also noted potential stakeholder interests extending beyond shareholders, including

- banks, financial institutions, and other organizations that lend funds;
- suppliers and others who provide credit, voluntarily or as unsecured creditors;
- customers, who rely on sustained performance of the company;
- partners, merger or joint-venture associates, and subsidiaries;
- market advisors, financial analysts, and underwriters;
- public accountants and lawyers who advise on commercial matters and can be drawn into dispute-management defensive roles;
- insurers and others who may warranty or indemnify performance;
- governors, both managers and directors, who can suffer financial and reputational losses, including from lost time and focus in disputes; and
- employees who rely on the sustained performance and reputation of the company.

To this list we would add the public interest.

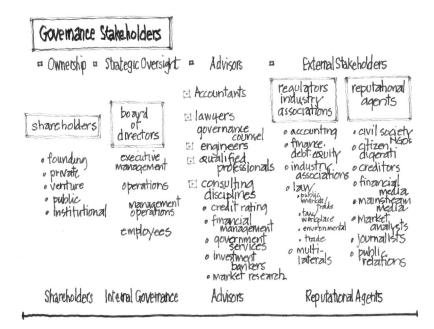

Thinking about what is *best* for any organization raises the question of what values apply, requiring that every organization prepare a vision or statement of foundational values or principles by which to weigh and rate priorities. Several values are common to most lists, such as effectiveness and accountability, integrity and transparency, and respect. Yet, many other values need to be concurrently engaged and actively reflected throughout the organization. For governance purposes, these are the meta-values needed to help identify conditions, organize principles, and reconcile standards. Several engage the concept of *best* as including a deliberative element, a step back to assess within the larger contexts and consequences.

There is also the traditional value of prudence, often forgotten in the rush of modern governance. Prudence should not be confused with an unthinking restraint or risk aversion. If prudence provides timely pauses in decisions, it is still relevant; if it unduly delays decisions it is not. It should respect, not constrain, fierce competition in the global marketplace, agile responses to opportunities, and crisis management.

The best-interests doctrine recognizes the fundamental strategic-oversight role of directors for good judgment on both fronts:

- strategic, to plan and set direction; and
- judicial, in oversight relative to such plans.

A best-interests analysis is at its core aspirational, forward thinking for risk and opportunity management. Although there is no general duty of good judgment, the duty to consider best interests is an important component under the rule of law. As an intangible, best interest is flexible over time and forever adaptable. It evolves to accommodate legal developments in the obligations and exercise of fiduciary or fiduciary-like duties such as the business-judgment presumption, entire-fairness reviews and oppression remedies.

In the kludge of shareholder values, social licenses, stakeholder interests, corporate purposes, marketing visions, and agreement objects, the duty to consider best interests provides an invaluable organizing principle.

Best-interests analysis will be increasingly important as hybrid organizations become more complex, and stakeholder interests and expectations increasingly receive greater public, investor and legal recognition. The language, principles, and practices of *best interests* in law have been tested in disputes for a century longer than *efficient-management practices* and a century and a half longer than *neuro-economics* (which looks at how economic decision-making actually happens inside the brain), yet each supports the other two in the emerging discipline of governance.

> The duty to consider best interests provides an invaluable organizing principle.

Principle 10: Choose Effectiveness Over Efficiency (Get the Right Things Done the Right Way)

What is the major problem? It is fundamentally the confusion between effectiveness and efficiency that stands between doing the right thing and doing things right.... There is surely nothing quite so useless as doing with great efficiency that which should not be done at all. Peter Drucker[8]

Prudence, due care, due diligence, best interests—an emphasis on continual learning—all these can be seen to urge the ambitious manager or director to get and stay busy at their governance tasks. But they all should come with a caution to avoid busyness for its own sake—to beware the sometimes indiscriminate promise of efficiency.

As Peter Drucker has noted, there is a potential tension between efficiency and effectiveness. The latter speaks to an evaluation of a decision, product, or performance outcome. Like efficiency, it might be positive or negative. In that, effectiveness is a *meta-value* for making sure our judgments are balanced. Strengths of organizational behavior, operational performance, and corporate culture are ways to measure business effectiveness. Governance effectiveness is measured by our capacity to align with best interests and other complementary values. Assessing effectiveness means evaluating our conduct or actions against values, principles, and standards of practice. We need to know what we are aspiring to in terms of our effectiveness—as an organization or as a director or manager. Being effective is a subset of accountability.

Beware the temptation to place efficiency in the short term in priority to effectiveness over time. The risks are that much may be done expediently, but the right things may not be done at all.

PART 4

Consequences

Accountability, Blame, Liability, and Conflicts of Interest

Accountability, responsibility, liability: these words can lurk like threats in the minds of new directors, especially if they have spent their time (wisely) learning about their duties before coming to a full understanding of their protections. In application, however, these are words and concepts that should be neutral. In principled governance, accountability should be seen as resolutely positive. Activated with integrity, it is a basic means of achieving, measuring, and evaluating success. If we account well for risks and variables, if we stand accountable to others, and if we hold to account whenever and wherever it is appropriate, there are benefits to be found in every direction.

In *principled* governance, there is also an implication, an expectation and, one hopes, an aspiration to moral behavior. That's why accountability and integrity are so often invoked together. Integrity, at the governance level, provides a moral underpinning for accountability. Properly harnessed, these two concepts can create a bias-free environment for critical thinking and decision-making. At the heart of the discussion of accountability and integrity—and the successful outcomes they may support—are aspiration and autonomy. Aspiration is what human beings hope and plan for: best outcomes. Autonomy is what human beings believe is the best way to achieve those aspirations: free will guided by access to the best information and guides (moral bases) available.

Inherent in the accountability framework, however, is the element that might justifiably give pause to the ill-prepared governor: consequences. There are *always* consequences for actions, good and bad. A well-built and carefully maintained system of accountability will help managers and directors anticipate, prepare for, and strategize around the most obvious outcomes. At times, however, when the systems of accountability are slow or broken—or the outcome are so unexpected as to be impossible to anticipate—we just have to face the consequences. And, for those times, we should be ready.

Blame and Liability

> I say that all men when they are spoken of... are remarkable for some of those qualities that bring them either blame or praise.... One is reputed generous, one rapacious; one cruel; one compassionate... one sincere, another cunning; one hard, another easy.... It would be most praiseworthy in a prince to exhibit all qualities that are considered good. But they can neither be entirely possessed nor observed, for human conditions do not permit it....
>
> And truly it is a very natural and ordinary thing to desire to acquire and always when men do it they will be praised or not blamed, but when they [try] and cannot herein lies the error and the blame.[1]—Niccolò Machiavelli, 1513

Machiavelli observed blame and praise, unaware that in the years to follow he would be blamed, then praised, then blamed, then praised and blamed. Now praised as a father of political science, and yet often blamed as having advanced pragmatism over morality, it's likely that if Machiavelli had survived to see the emergence of the modern rule of law, he would have pointed out that blame itself is an extreme reaction, sometimes merely unhelpful and sometimes a specific obstacle to fair and efficient review and reconciliation.

When accountability attracts consequences, in business as in life, we often characterize the result as *liability*. But it is important, in management and governance, to manage liability with dispassion and due process—and to beware the emotion and distraction of blame and outrage. It's important to distinguish between blame and liability and then to use these polarized influences to manage outrage and to navigate complex, sometimes contradictory parallel processes. In maintaining or enhancing internal accountability, it's also useful—perhaps essential—to facilitate anonymous reporting to identify potential governance issues, and to support smart regulation in managing issues when they arise. And, should all the foregoing fail, it's vital to learn when and how to apologize.

Blame and liability are *not* synonyms, even if they are both markers for unacceptable conduct: one according to personal norms, one according to social norms filtered through principles of law. Blame lives in the reptilian brain: it is instinctive, immediate, and accountable to personal values. Liability, on the other hand, is embedded in the rule of law: it is principled, accountable to group values, and results from due process, with consequences that are enforced. But the distinctions between the two can blur in the management suite or the boardroom, in the infinite challenges of self-interest, bias, informational asymmetry, cultural or professional differences and directors lawyering up to avoid personal liability. The swords and shields of our adversarial process were born in the time of Machiavelli, yet they survive with the advanced techniques of shotgun blame and in-house litigation squads. And this undermines good governance: pointing fingers in the boardroom generally flags uninformed or premature conclusions with negative attribution. Trouble is sure to follow.

> Blame lives in the reptilian brain; liability is embedded in the rule of law.

Blame

Blame is not a term of art in law. It is, rather, a cascade:

- a personal, emotional, and instinctive response;
- triggered when an error, accident, or danger occurs;
- resulting in condemnation for actions or inaction; and
- attribution to a perceived wrongdoer.

In this way, blame offers a simple narrative on how problems and tragedies arise and a beguilingly simple solution: sack, punish, excoriate the culprits.

But in governance, blame seldom helps. First, it is inclined to rest on personal judgments about what is morally right, a standard that's usually untested against organizational best interests or the rules of law. The act of blaming also tends to shut down inquiry; once a culprit is identified, people stop thinking seriously about contributing factors. It is sometimes easier (and more culturally acceptable) to blame than to fix.

Blame is also used as both a weapon and a shield. Blame takes an event and makes it personal, deflecting responsibility and undermining relationships. Those who are good at blaming may institutionalize blame to deflect personal accountability and avoid personal or institutional liability. Blame cultures flourish when the boss is jumping to conclusions, pursuing personal vendettas, and not learning or reconciling competing interests.

At the board level, some directors blame from ignorance, without information; others blame stupidly by ignoring available information. But among managers or directors, the instinctive and visceral reactions and the cognitive dominance of blame will become the default reaction unless lessons learned from law and equity are applied.

Further, there is the legal application of blame in rapid-fire shotgun litigation, which in effect blames everyone and everything. This can be formalized, random blaming or it might begin as a legal team's strategic attempt to identify all parties (and implicate the largest number of insurance companies) early in a litigation. Either way, it can create long-term damage that may or may not be resolved through normal, rule-of-law processes.

Blame can be mitigated, intuitively or intentionally. Intuitively, we tend not to blame who we like. Institutionally, blame can be mitigated by learning respect and disciplined accountability, especially if that tone is modeled high up in an organization.

Liability

Unlike blame, liability has a specific meaning in law: it is the obligation to others for goods, services or payment, conditions of restraint, or other conditions enforceable in law. A liability can be a debt, negotiated in good faith, or a penalty or compensation, owed by virtue of an action or inaction that caused damage to another. Unlike blaming, which can be knee-jerk and personal, liability provides an integrated, principled, and autonomous framework of enforcing conduct according to the rule of law.

If blame arises as the initial response to a negative incident, liability is established only after an assessment of accountability that weighs the values and standards of an organization or authority, the community of interest, familial traditions, belief systems, or personal networks. Legal liability is neither simple nor intuitive. It demands the organized reconciling of personal and public interests, and a proper process that can then enforce sanctions under statutory, regulatory, judicial, administrative, or contractual law.

There are also different kinds of liability:

- economic liability from exposure to long-term costs;
- financial liability from financial loss and damages;
- personal liability from loss of freedom;
- reputational liability from loss of status in the public eye;
- social liability from loss of cultural, social, or familial status or access to traditions; and
- environmental liability from loss of environmental integrity and vitality.

Liability's enforceability is largely a question of evidence, the establishment of which can be limited by processes, resources, and capacity. There are also practical differences between enforceable and enforcement: enforceable is having the right to enforce a legal decision; enforcement is getting the job done.

Ascertaining legal liability involves six steps:

- identifying the circumstances of an alleged breach;
- identifying what interests, rights, duties, and standards of conduct may apply among a variety of options and parallel processes;
- assessing whether a breach may have occurred;
- stating a claim, or alternative claims, for legal remedies;
- identifying causes;
- identifying whether defenses or special circumstances may apply; and
- assessing the detailed rules of evidence and procedure, including alternative dispute resolution for legal claims and proof of claims (evidence), for fairness and effectiveness, and costs of time and money to pursue.

This six-point assessment is also just the beginning. It is the due diligence required to confirm whether to initiate a legal process to establish liability, which, if successful, could secure a judgment for damages or recompense.

Where blame may be quick, liability can unfold extremely slowly. Even after a finding of legal liability, enforcement requires additional steps to realize penalties, restore damages or recover compensation—with potential appeals relating to process, fairness or legal interpretation.

For the director, there are also considerations of personal liability for breaches of fiduciary-like and statutory duties, including criminal, quasi-criminal, and extreme breaches of duties of care. Here again you find the risks of shotgun litigation: 90% of directors and managers in U.S. mergers and acquisitions expect to be sued (as distinct from "being found liable"). It is crucial, then, to understand directorial responsibilities beforehand. Avoidable problems arise when directors or officers don't know what they are expected to know, and are then blamed, held to account or face liability.

Fairness, Efficiency, and Time

In assigning blame or assessing liability, it is common for parties to urge "fairness" and prioritize "efficiency." But the perceptions of these can vary dramatically depending on personal values and on whether all parties have access to the same information.

There is also the always-pressing question of time: time to be informed, deliberative, and iterative, for both strategic and oversight decisions; and time for directors and managers to be on the same page for efficiency and accountability. Yet the constant search for "time efficiency" may itself apply pressure that results in errors, blaming and increased disputes.

So, take care to define shared and organizational interests and be reassured that the very act of collaborating in such a process can help mitigate liability risk. Collaborative cultures are better at collective problem solving, and better still when they have a tradition of accepting personal responsibility.

Outrage Management

Take a seed of blame layered with biases, withhold nourishing information, apply compressive stress and heat, and it only takes a New York minute for outrage to ignite.

In a digital environment in which the media and the public are quick to blame, companies and organizations face a heightened danger when they lack the skills of deliberative governance. The fast, often unmediated availability of information can provide a huge amount of "evidence" that serves principally as fuel for controversy.

Outrage itself is the collective response of individuals who are fueled by anger. And that anger can often be stoked by an asymmetry or asynchronicity of information. Information imbalances and gaps can be equally damaging within organizations or without.

Asymmetry can arise from actual differences in information flow, from vocational or cultural differences, from information bias, or even from a lack of agreed terms of reference. Asynchronicity is merely a question of timing; for example, as when management gets a piece of news first and acts on it without board input, creating the potential for misunderstanding (or, sometimes, charges of insider trading). Again, that raises the question of time, and especially making sure an organization has—and takes—the time to do due diligence, to question, and to clarify.

To the question of fast-flowing information being unmediated, this is a good example of words that require an agreed definition among directors and/or managers. Mediation, in law, describes a process of having a neutral third party assist in information flows between disputing parties. It is a common alternative dispute resolution (ADR) technique. But the root word, media, invokes a community of practitioners who use mediation to refer simply to the exchange of information, the purposes of which can range from the conscientious reporting of important information to the stirring of sensationalism or the purveying of entertainment. Just by interpreting the word "mediation" differently, one director might be expecting a communications game and another a sincere, interest-based process of resolving differences. It is important to be clear, especially when members of the media may be working not so much to inform as to tease out challenging or inflammatory views with no accountability for consequences.

It is also important, in the information gathering stage of any crisis or brewing dispute, to await fuller disclosure and embrace complexity. It's easy to be influenced by what is seen as tangible or simple, rather than picking through a thicket of facts and opinions that must be reconciled by disciplined study and strategic thinking.

Parallel Processes

We no longer live in the world of Machiavelli or at the time of the *Magna Carta,* when there were few arbiters of what was lawful. Today, panels of learned knights may appear on a spectrum of tribunals, regulatory agencies, or enforcement bodies. At any moment, an event may trigger interest from a host of courts or tribunals specialized by subject areas: corporate, tax, trade, strata or local community, immigration, or intellectual property. Such parallel processes create risks for multiple streams of blaming, claiming, corruption, compliance, defaming, framing—in civil law, criminal law, regulatory law, statutory law, and other public, private, or special interests.

It is not possible here to unravel or even fully describe all such processes, but the well-prepared director or manager must be alert to the existence and potential impacts of parallel processes and cross-triggering events, and be supportive of smart regulations to help navigate the tangle of influences, regulations, and laws.

It's also essential to be conscious of differing responsibilities: a manager needs to be compliance focused on what is possible today; a director needs to be looking at risks on the horizon. In walking the blame/liability tightrope, this presents a heightened challenge for the director: dispute-management theory was not a high business priority in the management era of market growth; and bonuses still depend more on quarterly success than on accountability for, or learning from, mistakes. The role of strategic oversight may now be more difficult and more important as a result.

Anonymous and Confidential Reporting

Gathering information effectively is fundamental to decision-making, particularly that which is necessary to comply with legal governance duties. The best way to avoid blame *or* liability is to anticipate and prevent, or at least prepare for, embarrassments or disasters. And complete, well-organized information is the best basis upon which to make best-interest analyses, to anticipate duties of care and to identify risks. This is especially true when the information is negative or critical—the kind of news that a manager might not want to hear, even if it is what he or she should be listening for most attentively.

Accordingly, every organization and management regime should make sure that the lines of communication are open and trusted. That often requires independent hotlines and support services that can invite and accommodate anonymous and confidential reporting. It is also important to avoid burdening that process with the pejorative language of whistleblowing. It is important to assure anyone who wants to contribute to continual improvement and accountability that their input is welcome and that they run no risk from passing on hard realities or bad news.

The Apology

In the world of blame and liability, the apology is often misunderstood, underutilized, and sometimes misused to negative effect.

A thoughtful apology has a meaningful impact when appropriate at any stage of negotiation, agreement, performance, or dispute management. It can be a vital step in getting back to business by focusing on being better informed, by narrowing issues, and expediting settlements. Offered sincerely and without ulterior motive, an apology can also drain the emotion—and the outrage—from a difficult situation, mitigating liability or, at least, smoothing the path to reconciliation.

Apologies can be misjudged—in their use and their impact. In the litigious modern era, overzealous advocates are inclined to wrongly assume that any public statement using language of apology is an admission of legal liability. The courts have not found it so. Apologies have also been scorned in competitive fields of advocacy or in adversarial boardrooms as signs of weakness. And apologies have been misused by those who expected an immediate resolution and abused as a kind of fairy dust by people trying to disorient an opponent at a critical juncture. It is equally wrong to use the apology as a hollow, proforma measure to avoid legal liability. That said, early apologies are increasingly expected by stakeholders in commercial cases—and thus likely to be favorably viewed in later assessments of legal liability.

> An apology need not be an admission of liability, but a sincere and respectful recognition—without prejudice—of damage done or felt.

An apology, sincerely and respectfully delivered, can bridge the accountability zone between instinctive blaming and principled systems of legal liability. Far from being a sign of weakness, an expression of regret can establish good faith and help to reset a difficult negotiation, discussion, or dispute resolution process. Apologies can also be iterative, with early expressions of regret being specific and discreet, and later apologies updated and clarified based on fuller information or on the formal determination of legal liability.

An apology requires important skills of respect and appreciation for the long-term importance of working with others in the complex cultural traditions of the marketplace. As such, every apology will be judged by its tone, tenor, content, and context. An insincere, remorseless, or stonewalling apology is more likely to inflame a situation that is, presumably, already difficult—and to invite blame, rather than promote an unemotional determination of liability.

Principle 11: Recognize and Manage Conflicts of Interest

Life is a conflict of interests. On a basic level, it's a conflict between time and demands for that time. On a more complex level, it is the conflict of allegiances, cultural biases, education, and self-interest. But these conflicts are not inherently bad. They're merely obstacles that we must recognize and navigate around as we pursue goals that are in the best interests of the organization.

As a matter of specific director or management liability, courts have been clear on the risks of conflicts of interest:

> He that is entrusted with the interest of others cannot be allowed to make the business an object of interest to himself, because of the frailty of nature one who has power will be too readily seized with the inclination to use the opportunity for serving his own interest....

> No fiduciary shall be allowed to enter into engagements with which he has or can have a personal interest conflicting, or which possibly may conflict with the interest of those he is bound to protect.[2]

> The general rule stands upon our great moral obligation to refrain from placing ourselves in relations which ordinarily excite a conflict between self-interest and integrity.... self-interest will exercise a predominant influence....[3]

> His duty calls upon him to act with the best interests of his principal; his self-interest prompts him to make the best bargain for himself. Humanity is so constituted that when these conflicting interests arise the temptation is too great to overcome and duty is sacrificed to [self] interest....[4]

But courts have also noted that there are no one-size-fits-all judicial cure: "One cannot pretend that there is any one consistent line of approach [to conflicts of interests] among different jurisdictions."[5]

Underlying the notion of conflict of interest is simply the default human condition of selfishness, or self-interest, which can be disruptive or harmful to productive effort. The problem is also magnified in the digital age. Technology increases the opportunities for bumping into people we do not know, or will not know well, and yet it also provides access for others to hold us accountable for conflicts, whether they arise from direct interests or from personal relationships, other business or professional relationships, and community relationships. So, while life is more complex—and while it may be increasingly difficult to see or understand our commonality of interests—our conflicts of interest become increasingly easy to see, for others if not for ourselves. This misalignment is the heart of the matter.

In governance, a surprising number of conflicts can be easily resolved, but problems concentrate in two broad areas:

- existing relationships, such as family or executive connections, and regulated insider or related parties; and
- any relationship that may influence, directly or indirectly, a manager or director's decision.

More specifically,

- if human instincts view and treat assets, funds, opportunities, relationships, and resources as limited for competitive advantage, or as finite pools, without a need to reconcile other interests; and
- if individuals do not learn and use executive skills of long-term, collaborative thinking to reconcile diverse interests; then
- people may be expected to default to self-preservation or self interest, especially if lines of accountability are unclear.

Conflict-of-interests policy should therefore focus on identifying personal or cultural bias, "because the brain cannot see itself fooling itself, the only reliable method for avoiding bias is to avoid the situations that produce it."[6]

In a global marketplace, the core concern is the effect of conflicts of interest on public confidence in markets, governments, and civil society; it is critical to align expectations and identify outdated practices to avoid decisions that are uninformed, inconsistent, and tainted of bias, perhaps leading to costly uncertainty.

Conflict of Interest—an Approach

The first step in a principled conflict framework is to remove the stigma. A conflict analysis need not impugn reputations. Rather, it should take inventory of relative interests, including relative duties and control. Conflict-of-interest standards should be clear in governance documents and directors should be given time to learn independent, deliberative, and principled judicial decision-making. Transparency and disclosure can go a long way in short-circuiting or avoiding the kind of high-profile problems that become media headlines and court cases.

Areas of Conflict

Historically, there are common areas in which conflicts of interest can be expected:

- conflicts among states (and conflicts of laws);
- conflicts among organizations (including state, civil society, and private organizations, whether adversarial, collaborative, or related);
- conflicts of individuals within public, private, civil society, or hybrid governance structures (directors and officers, shareholders and stakeholders); and
- conflicts among individuals' duties to or within faith, family, friends, and workplace (personal).

At the governance level, there are several other circumstances in which conflicts frequently arise, including

Conflicts of Self-Interest

Most obviously, when directors or managers have the opportunity to make a decision that affects their own financial well being, they should declare and, usually recuse.

Conflicting Interests of Director Time and Loyalty

An all-too common example of conflict arises among directors who are *over-boarded*—perhaps especially among those who flaunt a portfolio of active boards. The discipline for strategic oversight today demands time for due care in informed deliberation. Directors need time to receive, review, digest, update, inquire, understand, apply, and assess the sheer volume of information in governance. If directors spread themselves too thin, they may wind up slighting the interests of one organization in favor of fulfilling their responsibilities to another. Multiple and overlapping board appointments can also present directors with conflicts when two organizations are operating in the same space and their interests overlap or compete.

Concern also arises when certain directors are appointed by right of specialized legislation, by public-interest regulation, or by commercial agreement such as a debt financing or venture capital agreement. When these individuals retain interests back to their nominating or appointing party, they may lose focus on the best interests of the organization, inspiring suspicion and mistrust among other directors.

Conflicting Interests of Officer Control

Judges and regulators have identified conditions that present higher risks of conflicts becoming disputes, and nothing seems to trigger instinctive self-preservation in governance quite like a perception of impending loss of control. When ownership or shareholder control is in flux, managers and directors are often quick and collaborative in taking action to stay in charge, irrespective of stakeholder interests.

The case is seen most clearly in corporate takeovers. Boards and managers over the years have created a host of governance tools and legal devices that will protect their positions of control even in cases where there is no evidence this will benefit shareholders or the corporation at large. There are, for example, shareholder agreements or provisions with triggers known as poison pills that release new stock under conditions of a hostile proposed change of control. Managers and directors have also been known to negotiate golden parachutes in compensation agreements to soften the landing of executives after a merger-and-acquisition or reorganization.

Conflicting Shareholders' Interests

Directors also routinely make difficult decisions involving competing interests of various shareholder classes, even in cases where those directors hold one class of shares with preferential rights to another class. These conflicts are not automatically fatal, but that should offer no excuse to ignore fiduciary obligations to the corporation and all its shareholders.

Roles Matter: Never a Judge in One's Own Cause

A common factor in many disputes is the conflicts affecting those exercising judicial authority, or quasi-judicial evaluation, or strategic oversight. It is a basic principle in equity that no one judge their own cause or conduct. Problematic examples include:

- approving officers reporting to and paid by local governments, who have personal and vocational vested interests;
- strata-corporation managers who work for both developers and strata-councils;
- real-estate agents who act for more than one party in a transaction, or agents who acquire or option real-estate properties or interests in priority to a public offering; and
- any nominee director of a hybrid organization who is also a government employee of the nominating government.

Directors with experience in one sector sometimes need to unlearn and relearn the language of conflicts of interest for a new context or sector, to evaluate conflicts. Increasingly those individuals with the greatest mobility will encounter the most conflicting interests. It's crucial that they learn first principles *and* context-specific standards. Triggering events such as what is a gift or an acceptable standard of no-contact will change for those who move across or among businesses, publicly traded corporations, civil society or hybrid organizations, and regulators and public institutions.

The toolkit for mitigation may also vary, with boards having different standards for delegating functions, restricting access to information, enforcing recusal from discussion, decision, and oversight accountability.

The recusal is intended to mitigate the influence of the power of a personality in a conflict of interests. Yet, depending upon the circumstances and relative impacts, the mitigation may range from not voting to not being in the room to having no contact and receiving no information.

Independent Directors as a Guard Against Conflict

Independence is often waved about on the field of governance crisis. Yet, independence is neither required nor expected of all directors. It is a tool for reconciling interests, risks, and accountability.

Independence in governance is used in the context of fiduciary or fiduciary-like duties for those who hold the assets or lives of others in their hands. Traditionally, a strict fiduciary standard for independence was based on close relationships. Now, in addition to personal independence of relationships or bias, there is also structural independence in governance based on separating functions. Independence is not only a state of mind but of knowing and understanding what this means to the ongoing process of identifying risks.

While independent directors are assumed to inhibit management over-reach, there is little evidence that independent directors, acting alone, can have much effect as guards against conflict or arbiters of fairness in the face of management-controlled boards. Still, there is an increased acceptance and appreciation of what independent directors bring to a board. Advocates note that unbiased, impartial decision-making is more likely to be informed by active inquiry and oversight. Independent directors are assumed to bring more diverse points of view, standing alert to areas of conflict and filtering more effectively for gaps, risks, and opportunities. Public-interest regulators and institutional investors, seeking better risk management of public funds in the markets, are also requiring the appointment of a majority of independent directors for high-risk activities such as audit and compensation. Institutional investors, looking at the long-term, frequently require a minimum of three independent directors on boards looking for institutional investment.

Best-practice advocates in the post-Sarbanes-Oxley era recommended two-thirds of board directors be independent. However, independence needs to augment not replace executive directors. Fewer than three truly independent directors are unlikely to balance the weight of insider interests, but an obsession with independence can threaten organizational and sector intelligence, and, in the extreme, erode executive experience to respond to unforeseen risks and opportunities.

Reconciling executive and independent profiles particularly for hybrid organizations will produce the most resilient governance for the long-term.

A Conflicts Resolution

It's time to begin recognizing, formally, that conflicts of interest are generally common and often inevitable. Then we can proceed to mitigate, blamelessly, through proactive analysis and deliberative decision-making. Under the current practice, directors are assumed *not* to be in conflict unless they acknowledge or post a matter of concern. This is an unrealistic standard that serves mostly to undermine faith in the system—among governors, the media, and the public.

When asked, "Is there a conflict of interests?" it would be better for all to acknowledge that the answer at the first stage will usually be, "Yes"—an acknowledgment more in keeping public and media expectations. That, then, would trigger a blameless second stage requiring a deliberative review of the conflicts in question, the kind of process that would become faster and more efficient as systems are refined and more familiar.

This open and deliberative approach would assuage the notion of conflict as a stain or personal failing, identifying it more accurately as an attribute with possible risks to be mitigated in the complexity of the digital age.

A new conflicts-mitigation approach could also help overcome an endemic governance weakness. Historically, there has been too little formal training and too little attention to the governance role of strategic oversight, governance duties and doctrines such as conflicts of interests in law and equity. A formal process to acknowledge and mitigate conflicts of interest could help bridge gaps in governance-by-personality, bolstering organizational accountability, and market confidence. Conflict-of-interest programs could also stand as autonomous measures to identify and address human nature in the marketplace, and be applied across the spectrum of (a) early stage strategic thinking, (b) decision-processes, and (c) oversight.

Business schools have long recognized that successful managers benefit from well-defined systems and processes to help them get things done; we are only now coming to realize the importance of a governance discipline that gives directors the strategic-oversight practices necessary to get things done right. This starts with excellent board orientation, including statements of values, principles, and standards. The convergence of law, business, cognitive science, and technology points to the need for greater accountability and for objective, proactive conflicts analysis in governance.

PART 5

Summary

Principled Governance: An Emerging Discipline and an Essential Undertaking

Governance Framework

- The role of governance is strategic oversight.
- The core value of governance is respect.
- The core procedural duty is to ask questions.
- The core substantive duty is to reconcile best interests.

Governance Principles

Principle 1: Know Your Role
Principle 2: Choose Authority Over Power
Principle 3: Respect Complexity; Embrace Ambiguity
Principle 4: Act With Integrity; Welcome Accountability
Principle 5: Adopt Respectful Discourse and Civility
Principle 6: Beware Trust, Common Sense, and Loyalty (The Three Horsemen of the Governance Apocalypse)
Principle 7: Nurture Transdisciplinary Thinking
Principle 8: Take Time to Acquire Due Skill, and to Exercise Due Care and Due Diligence
Principle 9: Reconcile Best Interests
Principle 10: Choose Effectiveness Over Efficiency (Get the Right Things Done the Right Way)
Principle 11: Recognize and Manage Conflicts of Interest
Principle 12: Champion Principled Governance Leadership for Our Digital Age

We live in a time of ubiquitous information—and misinformation. This hyper-charged digital age has revealed a deficit in legal and governance literacy, even as it has given us a firehose flow of data that can inform or overwhelm, depending on our capacities and our level of preparedness. Indeed, our first—and unprecedented—challenge is staggering complexity. Digital logic has given us the means to assemble, organize, sort, and use massive amounts of information. This can allow directors and managers greater capacity to think about principles and protocols, to understand their own duties and to better oversee the successful operation of their organization. But the pressures of time and the challenge of complexity mean the governance task can no longer be regarded as intuitive. The skills must be learned.

> It is time to recognize governance as a separate discipline.

Consider the context. National boundaries blur with multilateral global organizations and unequal expectations from jurisdictions and regulators across the globe. Words can no longer be assumed to mean the same thing everywhere and, in the world of governance, the risk of misinterpretation is extraordinarily high. Operating within this diverse regulatory frame requires a shift to thinking about ideas and obligations, about patterns of difference, about risks and gaps.

As we look now towards learning the necessary literacy and skills, some governance activity is clear and well-defined—even if not always clearly understood among practitioners. Directors face legal duties to use due skill and due diligence. To that degree, the law demands that directors learn, or more often unlearn and relearn, what values, principles, and standards apply in the discipline of governance.

Along with managers, directors also bear responsibility for compliance in the face of regulation—which itself should be a neutral term. Like the rule of law—often within the rule of law—regulation has emerged as part of society's effort to manage complexity and reconcile interests. Good governance—principled governance—should be easier in a well-regulated global marketplace, but it will only be so if those responsible for governance understand their roles, their duties, their constraints, the values of their organization, and their responsibilities to reconcile interests, within and without.

In the business of management—and the management of business—the twentieth century might be recognized as a time of emerging professionalism in the executive suites of large corporations and front offices of small organizations of every type. Business schools brought research and rigor to the study and teaching of managerial skills and practice, and the benefit of that expanded knowledge flowed helpfully into a wider community. As the twenty-first century dawned, the same rigor—and benefit—could be seen emerging in the world of governance. Yet, five-hundred years after Machiavelli, the systems of director education, organization, and standards of conduct are still works in progress. It's time to fully face the risks and opportunities of the digital era and to meet the demands of governance education—and to begin by recognizing four imperatives.

The Role of Governance Is Strategic Oversight

Governance is a necessary collaboration of directors and managers. It is *not* management, and it is certainly not micromanagement, although many directors with an enthusiastic overconfidence of their expertise have made the mistake of overreaching into operations. The view, whether you are on a Fortune 500 corporate board or the executive council of a small residential strata, should be long term. Directors, working with senior managers, need to be looking for risks and gaps, and they need to be able to zoom in and out from local to global issues and concerns, and to anticipate, oversee, and assess patterns and to take the precautions and make the plans that will guide the organization to success. The two words define the task: strategic and oversight.

The Core Value of Governance Is Respect

In a discipline for the all too human, the core value of governance is respect: respect for the rule of law (and compliance!); respect for capacity constraints including clarifying roles such as between director and manager, and between the board chair and chief executive officer; respect for the time needed for learning governance skills, of information inventories, patterns, evaluation, and reconciliation; respect for the complexity of working within systems; and respect for managing personal biases and biases in others, in addition to understanding everyone's baseline interests and values.

The Core Procedural Duty Is to Ask Questions

Asking questions is a key role of any board member in exercising due diligence. It takes deep knowledge of an industry to ask technical questions, which often means that the first thing an alert director might ask is, "What do you mean by...?" Directors also need to maintain an independent perspective, to ask the tough governance questions—to throw light into the shadows and discomfit the sacred cows, to help everyone at the table fulfill the duties and enjoy the benefits of informed strategic oversight.

The Core Substantive Duty Is to Reconcile Best Interests

To an extent unprecedented in history, the digital age has given us the tools and information to identify best interests—of our own organizations and of the communities, local and global, where we operate—and to reconcile those interests to best collective effect. The health and welfare of our organization depends, ultimately, on the continued health, safety, sustainability, and prosperity of the environments in which we exist and operate. The long view, the attitude of respect, and the care and diligence exercised in our own milieu are the best contribution good governors can make to the best interests of the whole.

Principled Governance; Governance Principles

Principle 1: Know Your Role

This is the best advice for every new director and, too often, the best reminder for seasoned directors: Know your role. If you find yourself on a board or governing council, you almost certainly were recruited or elected thanks to some fortuitous mix of skill and knowledge, but even more for your ability to listen, to learn, and to exercise strategic judgment. "Know your role" is also apt advice for managers, who must remember to rise above their appropriately focused day-to-day concerns when working with their boards on governance tasks.

In simple terms, managers or members of the executive must focus their attention on the details of daily operations and performance with a pragmatic priority on the short-term and on the well-being of the organization. Directors are responsible for strategic oversight—the longer-term, strategic context—with periodic review and input. While respecting short-term needs, directors must work with managers to plan, prepare, watch for trouble and reconcile complex interests for the best interest of the organization.

To say again, the primary role for directors, always, is strategic oversight. Directors are never recruited to micromanage. Even if they feel they bring appropriate managerial qualifications, it is simply not their job. Management may benefit from their advice and insight, but directors must be careful to limit actual *direction* to matters of oversight and long-term strategy. Directors and managers need to respect and understand each other's roles and to work collaboratively.

Principle 2: Choose Authority Over Power

Directors newly installed in a position of authority need to understand the source of that influence, treat it respectfully, and avoid willful displays of power that can be disruptive and counterproductive to the effectiveness of a well-functioning board.

Legal authority in governance is essentially the right to make decisions. It is based on the laws, rules, regulations, and conventions of the organization in question. Another concept often paired with authority is power. Although the two words are often used synonymously in law and business, there are clear differences:

- Power arises from the people involved; authority is born of the rule of law.
- Power focuses on an individual and dies with the individual; authority focuses on context within a group and sustainable frameworks.
- Power is taken or assumed; authority is granted by another.

In the time of Machiavelli and before, the ability to govern was rooted in power: people accepted decisions because a prince or governor had the capacity to force them to do so. Today, after 5 centuries of development in the rules of law, we now have a collectively authorized framework to enable diverse groups of people to build and manage organizations, marketplaces, and communities, effectively.

There likely will always be people with the physical or intellectual power to, metaphorically at least, throw their weight around. All those involved in principled governance should question why they should.

Principle 3: Respect Complexity; Embrace Ambiguity

We live in an impossibly complex age. On any particular day, dealing with any particular issue, there may be too many moving parts, too many competing interests, and too much contradictory information. It is increasingly necessary, in exercising strategic leadership and oversight, to learn how to hold and be comfortable with ambiguity until due diligence or time constraints warrant otherwise.

Acknowledging complexity does not imply surrender or any abdication of the responsibility to understand and search for effective solutions. Complexity should not be used as an excuse for delay or dithering. Rather, it calls for prudence in understanding what is to be decided and in providing or moderating courage in action.

There is also a huge risk in *rejecting* ambiguity in a complex situation: The simple solution is so often, simply, ineffective. When you have taken action, there is a further risk that you will regard the problem as solved and stop paying attention—perhaps missing a second wave until it overwhelms.

Increasingly, complexity is resolved not through solution but by accommodation. Sometimes, the best you can do is learn to live with a certain amount of doubt and unpredictability. So, when an answer to a complex problem seems easy or obvious, be skeptical. Be respectful. Be patient. In an irresolvable situation, embracing ambiguity may be your best defense.

Principle 4: Act With Integrity; Welcome Accountability

Since the time of Adam Smith, there has been a happy delusion that self-interest alone will moderate markets and human affairs. Three centuries of history, however, have shown that we very much need the instruments and benefits of good and principled governance, exercised with restraint and integrity.

The latter is tricky. Although the most commonly cited morally desirable trait in business and government, integrity is neither a classically defined moral virtue, nor a concept that is systematically applied. At the core of integrity is the idea of consistency—or constancy. This does not imply behavior that is static or inflexible: People with integrity may be agile, respectful of diversity, and at ease with randomness and ambiguity. Rather, integrity promises predictable fealty to the fiduciary triad of best interests, good faith, and honesty.

If you are acting with integrity, you might readily welcome accountability. Certainly, there is only risk in trying to evade it. The minute you step into a governance chair, you *are* accountable, which sometimes also means being legally liable. It's best to recognize and embrace that fact, tracking risk in a way that creates an area of strength, not an avenue of risk.

Accountability is defined as a process identifying responsibility, conditions, contingencies, and costs or benefits associated with an act, event, or omission. Being accountable doesn't imply that you're likely to get into trouble; rather, welcoming accountability and demanding it around you is the best way to prevent trouble from occurring in the first place.

Principle 5: Adopt Respectful Discourse and Civility

Civility, with common roots like civil and civic, is all about people coming together for common interests. The call for civility—in governance if not in all of society—is tied to a core value of being respectful and observant of all governing protocols, laws, traditions, and practices. This imperative is all the greater in a global marketplace in which dozens of languages may be spoken in a single elementary school. We need to refine governance literacy for both vocational and cultural understanding.

Learning civility is a great place to start. And civility is assuredly learned, not inherited or inherent. One cannot assume that people will come to a board without inherent bias or places of intellectual comfort. Individuals may then default to their biases during times of stress or decision making unless they have intellectual tools to do otherwise. Teaching civility means assessing risks of inherent bias/comfort, understanding empathy, and maintaining open mindedness during times of crisis.

Civility is the foundation for collaboration and deliberative dialogue to reconcile interests, and collaboration and deliberative dialogue lead to better board performance and outcomes. The willingness to learn can also overcome confusion that is buried in language or culture.

Civil conduct reconciles values, principles, standards, matters, issues, problems, and disputes. Intolerance, on the other hand, increases risk.

Principle 6: Beware Trust, Common Sense, and Loyalty (The Three Horsemen of the Governance Apocalypse)

Among the values or constructs long revered in Western society, trust, common sense, and loyalty have been defining. But the real value in trust comes not from being trusting—which may be a synonym for naïve—but from being trustworthy. To be positive, trust must be earned, not given. Loyalty, as well. It might be appropriate that a leader, a manager, or a brand might command loyalty, but only after having won it through excellent performance. To *demand* loyalty is something different. And what of common sense? On its face, it means assenting to what *I* assume to be true, righteous, moral, and sensible. But it triggers the question: "Common to whom?" In a diverse world, a manager or director is best to avoid believing that their own views are commonly held. It's best to check.

Yet the imperatives of trust, common sense and loyalty have long been invoked to legitimize the ignoring, dismissing, minimizing, or denigrating of others and of their perceptions, experiences, values, interests, and concerns. They privilege the biases, prejudices, and worldview of self over other. These same constructs perpetuate authority in the hands of the few and allow those few to continue to privilege a narrow set of preconceptions and priorities.

By all means, aspire to be trustworthy. Do all you can to inspire loyalty. And do the research you must to understand as best you can the public consensus. Just don't assume that any of these comes to you by right.

Principle 7: Nurture Transdisciplinary Thinking

We come again to the Mandarin proverb, *Huó dào lǎo, xué dào lǎo*—"You are never too old to learn, and you can never know enough." It is impossible in the digital age, when we have access to more information than we can digest or understand, to fully inform ourselves. In the context of a modern board, where directors must sort out the complexities of finances, law, operations, risks, and opportunities, we can never know enough—so we need to know who does. That's why a well-balanced board will have a diversity of subject area experts. It's also why we all need to nurture the skills of transdisciplinary thinking.

To understand transdisciplinary, consider the definition of interdisciplinary, which requires that we can work with other disciplinary experts on complex projects. This means recognizing expertise and trusting the skills, knowledge, and, sometimes, wisdom of experts outside our own fields.

Yet, it's not enough, in principled governance, to accept the advice of others as if it were delivered from some impenetrable black box. Transdisciplinary thinking does not require that you become an expert in everything. But it implies a heightened degree of attention when you are working outside, or at the edge of, your own area. It means that instead of tuning out during the report from a special committee outside your field, that you should be listening harder. You need to learn enough to understand what you don't know; that's where you'll find all the good questions.

Principle 8: Take Time to Acquire Due Skill, and to Exercise Due Care and Due Diligence

Since the first Watergate investigator asked the question, "What did the president know and when did he know it?"—there has been a mistaken impression that ignorance of the law is actually a pretty good excuse. That is, if you could argue that you weren't in the loop, you might also make the case that you weren't responsible; you certainly couldn't be blamed in the cover-up. Yet, as a risk-management strategy, hiding in ignorance is a defensive strategy almost perfectly designed to get you into more trouble. Ignorance is *not* bliss. You can't protect yourself against risks you can't see. You have a practical, moral, and legal duty of care.

The duty of care is a label used to bundle several component duties, the legally enforceable obligations to use due skill, due care, and due diligence measured by the standards of the day:

- *Due skill* is learned knowledge and technique, currently including the obligations for continual updating of strategic oversight and judgment skills.
- *Due care* is taking the time to be informed, reflect, and consider, including the obligation to establish internal controls.
- *Due diligence* is persistence in inquiry, knowing the importance of being informed, and using internal controls to do so.

So, make sure that you or someone on your board has the knowledge and accreditations you collectively need and that you are, generally, taking care. And then ask questions, persistently: ultimately, it's the only way you'll know.

Principle 9: Reconcile Best Interests

Modern managers and directors operate in a blizzard of self-interest, special interests, public interests, and private interests. The challenge in principled governance is to find a better filter—a system of analysis that will identify and try to deliver on the best interests of all those who are involved or affected.

The best-interests doctrine captures the need to identify relevant interests, identify organizational priorities and contexts, and reconcile the different interests involved. It anticipates identifying a broad set of relevant organizational interests, including those of shareholders or members, management, and employees, as well as commercial, special, and public interests.

When directors come from diverse backgrounds, education, experience, and expectations, they may lack a clear understanding of their role or of governance duties in law, and they may not yet have the skillset for strategic oversight. The best-interest approach started with an innovative tool: the legal interest—an enforceable legal right. As an analytical unit, it is intangible, but flexible and scalable from self-interest to special interests to public interests. The start in any best-interest analysis is therefore to cast the net widely to identify and organize a baseline inventory of interests.

The skills and knowledge required to analyze best interests are fundamental for good governance yet need to be learned. It is not easy to set aside self-interest and special interests. Exercising good judgment reconciles complex interests for the long term, but this is not something most people do often. In governance, it is expected—and required.

Principle 10: Choose Effectiveness Over Efficiency (Get the Right Things Done the Right Way)

The management consultant and author Peter Drucker once asked, rhetorically, "What is the major problem (in business)?" His answer: "It is fundamentally the confusion between effectiveness and efficiency that stands between doing the right thing and doing things right.... There is surely nothing quite so useless as doing with great efficiency that which should not be done at all."[1]

There is, in almost every organization, a potential tension between efficiency and effectiveness. The former reflects best the modern anxiety to get things done quickly with minimal fuss. The latter speaks to an evaluation of a decision, product, or performance outcome. Effectiveness is a meta-value for making sure our judgments are balanced.

Consultants are forever trying to measure business effectiveness on the strengths of organizational behavior, operational performance and corporate culture. And we measure governance effectiveness by our capacity to align with best interests and other complementary values. Assessing effectiveness means evaluating our conduct or actions against values, principles and standards of practice. We need to know what we are aspiring to—as an organization or as a director or manager—before we can assess whether we are being effective.

So, beware the risk of prioritizing efficiency in the short term over effectiveness over time. The risks are that much may be done well, but the right things may not be done at all.

74 ▪ *Principled Governance When Everything Matters*

Principle 11: Recognize and Manage Conflicts of Interest

Life is a conflict of interests. It is a conflict between time and demands for that time, and it is full of conflicts of allegiance, cultural biases, education, and self-interest. But these conflicts are not inherently bad. They're merely obstacles that we must recognize and navigate around as we pursue goals that are in the best interests of the organization.

Underlying the notion of conflict of interest is the default human condition of selfishness, or self-interest, which can be disruptive or harmful to productive effort. Technology also increases our exposure and, potentially, our areas of interest, even as it provides access for others to hold us accountable for conflicts, whether they arise from direct interests or from personal relationships, other business or professional relationships, or community relationships. So, while it may be increasingly difficult to see or understand our commonality of interests, others can more easily recognize when our interests conflict. Here lies misunderstanding and risk.

An effective framework for managing conflicts of interest need not be stigmatizing. Rather, it should take inventory of relative interests, including relative duties and control, and then set out mechanisms to control for or mitigate the effects of any conflict. Standards should be clear in governance documents and directors should be given time to learn independent, deliberative, and principled judicial decision-making. Transparency and disclosure can also help short-circuit or avoid the kind of high-profile problems that become media headlines and court cases.

Principle 12: Champion Principled Governance Leadership for Our Digital Age

At the beginning of the sixteenth century, Niccolò Machiavelli looked unsentimentally at the state of governance and concluded that, in a world of ruthlessness, selfishness, violence, and dishonesty—a world without the rule of law—the successful governor would sometimes have to be ruthless, selfish, violent, and dishonest. More precisely, Machiavelli prescribed "force, fortune, and *virtu*," which were translated to mean: power and the ability and willingness to wield it; uncertainty (where fortune is understood more as chance than as wealth) and the ability to overcome;

and, with *virtu,* a kind of wary cleverness. He advised princes that it was "safer to be feared than loved," and for having done so, he is now remembered as an amoral pragmatist whose very name rings of political cynicism.

Yet, in the modern age—in which governance is now bolstered by a rule of law that has developed over many centuries—it is surely appropriate to be guided more by civil Machiavelli's aspirations than by the cold realities of his bygone era. He said, "Nothing brings a man greater honor than the new laws and institutions he establishes, when they are soundly based and bear the mark of greatness." And, "Nothing makes a prince so much esteemed as great enterprises and setting a fine example."

The world of governance has evolved to include the organizational architecture necessary to build great enterprises. And the rule of law has developed to protect those who set a fine example and to punish those who do not. A great opportunity lies before us.

But Machiavelli also wrote, "The human tragedy is that circumstances change, but man does not." Some might use this as an argument to get more women appointed to boards and senior management (which should be a given), but the central message might be that good governance—principled governance—is up to you. Governance will not be transformed by people standing on the sidelines or by cleaving to the standards that Machiavelli observed with such caution. In this digitally amplified, digitally accelerated age—an age when everything is accessible and *everything matters*—a successful shift to principled governance will require a new generation of managers and directors who learn, grasp, and implement the principles enunciated here.

You have taken the first step. May you find success and fulfillment in the steps to come.

Biography of David S. Fushtey

DAVID STEWART FUSHTEY
AUGUST 21,1955 | OCTOBER 8, 2019

David S. Fushtey (1955–2019) was an expert in the governance of conventional and hybrid boards and councils, and especially in the continuing challenge of balancing private and public interests. In his career, he worked in international corporate-commercial law, developing a principled governance approach to help balance comparative best practices in corporate and regulatory compliance, and in civil-society organizations. His conclusions on the strategic-oversight role of directors and managers in interdisciplinary governance were informed by his fifteen years as a governance specialist, but equally by his formative experience as an oil-rig roughneck, construction-operations manager, world's fair planner and planning commission chairman, economic-policy forum chair, and by a decade as an international corporate-commercial lawyer.

Dave was a Fellow of the American Bar Foundation, past Senior-Fellow of the Centre for Corporate Governance and Risk Management, and past Fellow of the Centre for Dialogue, SFU Vancouver. He served with the American Bar Association International Law section and was interim chair of an international resource-development enterprise, and he spent twenty-five years in law and governance focused on international commercial transactions and hybrid-enterprise development, with particular reference to governance duties.

Engaging others in the role of law in governance, Dave was a frequent seminar leader and lecturer in myriad academic settings and a popular keynote speaker before boards of directors and governance professionals and organizations of all kinds.

Notes

Note: For detailed citations refer to *The Director and the Manager: Law and Governance in a Digital Age: Machiavelli Had It Easy* by David S. Fushtey (2019, Information Age Publishing).

Prologue: Since Machiavelli: Times Have Changed; People, not so Much

1. Niccolò Machiavelli, *The prince* (Chicago: University of Chicago Press, 1998), c. III 15. Originally published in ca. 1513
2. Niccolò Machiavelli, *Il principe* (Oxford: Oxford University Press, 2005), c.XVII.
3. Machiavelli, *Il principe*, 2005 c.XVII.
4. Conrad Black, *A Matter of Principle* (Toronto: McClelland & Stewart, 2011).
5. Black. p. 62
6. Machiavelli, *Il principe*, 2005 c.XVII.
7. Pasteur, L. *Lecture*, University of Lille, Lille, France. December, 1854.
8. Niccolò Machiavelli, and Ninian Hill Thomson, *Discourses on the first decade of Titus Livius* (London: K. Paul, Trench & Co., 1883).
9. Machiavelli, *Il principe*, 2005.
10. Aurelius, M. (2003). *Meditations* (G. Hays, Trans.). London, England: Weidenfeld & Nicolson.
11. Machiavelli, *Il principe*, 2005.
12. Machiavelli, *The prince*, 1998 cs.xvii, xxi.
13. Machiavelli, *Il principe*, 2005 C.VI.
14. Niccolò Machiavelli, *The prince* (Chicago: University of Chicago Press, 1998), *cs.xvii, xxi*. Originally published in ca. 1513

15. Niccolò Machiavelli, *The prince* (Chicago: University of Chicago Press, 1998), c. XXVI Originally published in ca. 1513

Part 1: Governance in the Digital Age

1. Niccolò Machiavelli, *The prince* (Chicago: University of Chicago Press, 1998), c. XXVI Originally published in ca. 1513
2. Adrian Cadbury, *Report of the committee on the financial aspects of corporate governance (Cadbury Report)* (2000), retrieved from www.ecgi.org/cordes/documents/cadbury
3. Jay W. Lorsch, Joseph L. Bower, Clayton S. Rose, and Suraj Srinivasan, *Perspectives from the Boardroom—2009* (Boston, MA: Harvard Business School Working Paper, 2009), retrieved from https://hbswk.hbs.edu/item/perspectives-from-the-boardroom-2009
4. IOSCO and OECD, *The Application of Behavioural Insights to Financial Literacy and Investor Education Programmes and Initiatives*, 2018.
5. Economist Intelligence Unit, 2014, retrieved from www.eiu.com

Part 2: Governance Beyond Machiavelli

1. Rule of Law, Oxford English Dictionary online, accessed September 13, 2018.
2. Principled, Oxford English Dictionary on-line, accessed September 9, 2020.
3. Robert Audi and Patrick E. Murphy, *The Many Faces of Integrity*, Business Ethics Quarterly, 2006, 16(1), 3–21.
4. Norman P. Griffith (et al.), *The Charm Offensive: Cultivating Civility in 21st Century Britain*, retrieved from https://www.youngfoundation.org/publications/charm-offensive-cultivating-civility-in-21st-century-britain/
5. Keith Roberts, *The Origins of Business, Money, and Markets* (New York, NY: Columbia Business School Publishing, 2011), 149.
6. The Economist, *Attitude to Business: Milton Friedman goes on tour*, retrieved on 09/06/20 https://www.economist.com/business/2011/01/27/milton-friedman-goes-on-tour

Part 3: Risk, Diligence, and Best Interests

1. Autem Nicomachus Aristotle, *Nicomachean ethics* (David W. Ross, Trans. 1925), ca 350BCE, III, 5.iii.
2. Alexandra Reed-Lajoux and Charles Elson, The art of m&a due diligence (New York, NY: McGraw-Hill, 2000), 4.
3. J. C. Smith and Peter Burns, *Donoghue v. Stephenson: The not so golden anniversary*, Modern Law Review, 1983, 46 (2), 147–163.
4. Brian R. Cheffins, *The history of modern U.S. corporate governance* (Cheltenham: Edward Elgar, 2011), xvi.

5. Robert A. G. Monks and Nell Minow, *Corporate governance* (5th Ed), (West Sussex: John Wiley, 2011).
6. Carol Hansel, Corporate governance: what directors need to know (Toronto: Thompson Carswell, 2003), 117.
7. Caremark International Inc. Derivative Litigation. Civil Action No. 13670 (Court of Chancery of Delaware, New Castle County, 1996), *Del SC 1996, 969.*
8. Peter F. Drucker, *The essential Drucker: Writings on Management* (New York, NY: Harper Business, 2001), 20.

Part 4: Consequences

1. Niccolò Machiavelli, *The prince* (Chicago: University of Chicago Press, 1998), c. III 15.
2. *Aberdeen Railway v. Blaikie,* UK HL 1854, 461.
3. *Michoud v. Girod,* US 1846, 554.
4. *Pacific Vinegar and Pickle Works,* US SCCal, 1908, 366.
5. *CanAero,* 1974, 612.
6. Daniel Gilbert, *I'm okay, you're biased.* New York Times, 2006, retrieved 09/06/20, https://www.nytimes.com/2006/04/16/opinion/im-ok-youre-biased.html

Part 5: Summary

1. Drucker, *The essential Drucker: Writings on Management,* 20.

CPSIA information can be obtained
at www.ICGtesting.com
Printed in the USA
BVHW040544090921
616403BV00013B/76